WordPress for

Kids

A Creative Book for Kids to Master WordPress, Its Themes, and Plugins with Complete Fun

D. S. Aman

www.bpbonline.com

FIRST EDITION 2022

Copyright © BPB Publications, India

ISBN: 978-93-55510-440

LIMITS OF LIABILITY AND DISCLAIMER OF WARRANTY

To View Complete
BPB Publications Catalogue
Scan the QR Code:

Dedicated to

My beloved Grandparents:
Shri Bir Bhadra Mishra
Smt Madhavi Mishra
Whose blessings continue to
guide me even in their absence.

About the Author

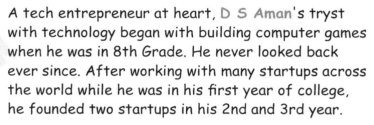

A tech entrepreneur at heart, D S Aman's tryst with technology began with building computer games when he was in 8th Grade. He never looked back ever since. After working with many startups across the world while he was in his first year of college, he founded two startups in his 2nd and 3rd year.

His recent success was HighApe that became a multi-million dollar business and India's leading experience discovery platform. Aman has also worked as Consulting CTO for early-stage Blockchain and Ed-Tech startups, helping them build and scale their business globally. He has even enabled thousands of students to enter the field of web development through his courses on Udemy and his YouTube channel.

Currently, he is the Head of Product and Technology for a new disruptive eyewear business vertical at Lenskart, thereby taking eyewear access to the next 500 million Indians.

About the Reviewer

Vaibhav Lall is a storyteller in many avatars, be it writing a fictional manuscript or scrapping out a multi-million dollar entrepreneurial venture from scratch.

The journey began in 2011 with a freelance writing project for some extra pocket money, and the spark deftly transformed into an endless affair with wordplay and the magic it withholds. Leading the editorial board in early-stage startups – Rise for India, HighApe, and Top Brands and Products, Vaibhav assimilated the nuances and intricacies of multiple writing styles and formats.

Currently, his team at Cuemath – a google backed ed-tech company – is channeling the creative energy towards dishing out the best content pieces for its global audience.

Being fortunate enough to do what he loves the most as a 'full-time job,' coming from an engineering background, Vaibhav fancies the power of storytelling.

Acknowledgement

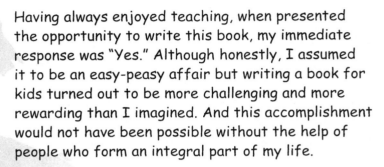

Having always enjoyed teaching, when presented the opportunity to write this book, my immediate response was "Yes." Although honestly, I assumed it to be an easy-peasy affair but writing a book for kids turned out to be more challenging and more rewarding than I imagined. And this accomplishment would not have been possible without the help of people who form an integral part of my life.

I would first like to thank my parents and sister for always believing in me and for their constant motivation whenever I took the plunge to try something new. Instead of putting the brakes on for things that admittedly were sometimes stupid, they always took pride and motivated me to reach new heights.

I would also like to thank many of my friends who have always been around. My college friends, especially Abhishek Sharma, who helped me cope with my college studies while I was lost in the fantasy world of technology and startups. My school friends, Vaibhav Lall and Prasun Kumar, who joined me in my journey of building startups, which enabled me to learn so much about different technologies. And Ankita Singh, who always stood firmly by my side, providing unwavering support.

Last but not least, I would also like to express my gratitude to the BPB Publications for providing me this opportunity.

Preface

This book covers the exciting technology of WordPress that powers more than 40% of websites on the Internet. With simple steps, a lot of screenshots, and real-world examples, this book makes it very easy for kids to start making websites using WordPress.

The book takes a practical approach toward website development. As we move forward in the book, we start creating a website of our own, which we keep improving with each chapter. By the end of the book, we create a beautiful website with a lot of features and functionalities.

The book is divided into 18 chapters. Each chapter covers an aspect of WordPress that would assist us in understanding this technology better. The details of the chapters are listed as follows:

Chapter 1 will be an introductory chapter to familiarize with WordPress, and gain an intuitive understanding of this technology. With the help of Subway Sandwiches, we will understand what WordPress is and why it is so useful for building websites. We will also see a few major websites based on WordPress, which will further motivate us to learn this CMS system.

Chapter 2 will guide the readers to create their account on wordpress.com using multiple login methods on the website. We will set a name for the website, complete the basic configuration, and explore the various options available on the dashboard. We will understand the purpose of a dashboard and how it will help us build our website without writing any code!

Chapter 3 will cover User management features on WordPress, which will provide us control over our website. We will learn, step by step, how to add our friends and family to the WordPress dashboard so that they can work alongside us to help us out. We will explore different levels of permissions and what they are meant for.

Chapter 4 will cover a few basic terminologies that are very common in the field of web development. We will explore terms like Header, Footer, Menu, Body, and Hyperlinks. We will use various analogies in this chapter to easily understand the meaning of these terms.

Chapter 5 will cover Posts & Pages - the two main ways to create content on a WordPress website. We will learn the difference between the two and when to use these. We will explore this concept with the help of the school timetable analogy, thus making it easier to understand.

Chapter 6 will detail out various options available on the dashboard for creating posts. We will cover, step by step, how to create a Post on WordPress.

Chapter 7 will cover comments, categories, and tags. Although comments will help us enable discussion with our website visitors, categories and tags will make it easier for us to categorize content on our website so that it is easier for our website visitors to find them.

Chapter 8 will explain different steps to follow for creating a Page on WordPress.

Chapter 9 will cover Themes - the most important part to make our website look beautiful. We will gain an intuitive understanding of Themes with the help of examples.

Chapter 10 will explain various options available to us for customizing the design of our website. We will cover each option and see how to customize it to make our website look more beautiful.

Chapter 11 will introduce the concept of Menus with the help of maps. We will also learn how to create Menus on WordPress websites.

Chapter 12 will cover Widgets and we will also learn how to add custom content blocks to our website to make it look more enriched.

Chapter 13 will cover the benefits of going for a paid plan. We will also learn how to upgrade our plan to avail those benefits.

Chapter 14 will cover the concept of Plugins. We will learn what plugins are capable of and why we should use them. We will cover how to search plugins and choose the ones that will help us add the required features to our website.

Chapter 15 will introduce us to Search Engine Optimization or SEO. We will use the Yoast SEO plugin to optimize the content on our website for search engines.

Chapter 16 will help us understand how to add animation to our website to make it look more interactive.

Chapter 17 will cover a few more plugins, such as those for adding popups and WhatsApp chat features on our website.

Chapter 18 will explain what can be done next after completing the book in our web development journey.

Coloured Images

Please follow the link to download the
Coloured Images of the book:

https://rebrand.ly/0ee40e

We have code bundles from our rich catalogue of books and videos available at **https://github.com/bpbpublications**. Check them out!

Errata

We take immense pride in our work at BPB Publications and follow best practices to ensure the accuracy of our content to provide with an indulging reading experience to our subscribers. Our readers are our mirrors, and we use their inputs to reflect and improve upon human errors, if any, that may have occurred during the publishing processes involved. To let us maintain the quality and help us reach out to any readers who might be having difficulties due to any unforeseen errors, please write to us at :

errata@bpbonline.com

Your support, suggestions and feedbacks are highly appreciated by the BPB Publications' Family.

Did you know that BPB offers eBook versions of every book published, with PDF and ePub files available? You can upgrade to the eBook version at www.bpbonline.com and as a print book customer, you are entitled to a discount on the eBook copy. Get in touch with us at :

business@bpbonline.com for more details.

At **www.bpbonline.com**, you can also read a collection of free technical articles, sign up for a range of free newsletters, and receive exclusive discounts and offers on BPB books and eBooks.

Piracy

If you come across any illegal copies of our works in any form on the internet, we would be grateful if you would provide us with the location address or website name. Please contact us at **business@bpbonline.com** with a link to the material.

If you are interested in becoming an author

If there is a topic that you have expertise in, and you are interested in either writing or contributing to a book, please visit **www.bpbonline.com**. We have worked with thousands of developers and tech professionals, just like you, to help them share their insights with the global tech community. You can make a general application, apply for a specific hot topic that we are recruiting an author for, or submit your own idea.

Reviews

Please leave a review. Once you have read and used this book, why not leave a review on the site that you purchased it from? Potential readers can then see and use your unbiased opinion to make purchase decisions. We at BPB can understand what you think about our products, and our authors can see your feedback on their book. Thank you!

For more information about BPB, please visit **www.bpbonline.com**.

Table of Contents

Structure Bot

In this chapter, we will discuss the following topics:

◆ Factors to consider before you start building your website

◆ Understanding different ways of building websites

◆ Basics of servers, frontend, and backend

◆ What is WordPress?

◆ Major websites built using WordPress

Although web development is my daily routine, I am still in awe every time my team creates a working web product. I find the art of creating websites and web applications exhilarating. The power of creating something new that adds value to the world is tremendous. It is like a fantasy world where you get a chance to play God with complete freedom.

You can do anything. Want to open up a store? Create an e-commerce website. Saw a problem in issuing books in your library? Create a library management system.

The power is insane. And as adults, as much as we enjoy and boast about it, this power can only amplify in the hands of kids. A few days ago, I watched this series on *Netflix* called *"The Dragon Prince"*. The King in the series says to his son:

"The great illusion of childhood is that adults have all the power and the freedom. But the truth is the opposite. A child is freer than a king."

That is 100% true. And with technology, this has become more possible than ever before! Not only are kids freer today, but they can leverage the power of the Internet to create things that most adults can only dream of. So get ready to be awed by your own creations like the girl in the following *Figure 1.1*, as you gain the power of building websites:

Figure 1.1: *A girl looking at her laptop*

Yes, it is time for kids to turn the table and unleash their creativity to create some amazing products, which would make the world a better place. And that is what this book is going to teach you. We are together going to learn how to build websites from scratch. What you create with the knowledge provided in this book – we will leave that totally up to you because the possibilities are limitless!

 *Objective Bot*

At the end of this chapter, you will:

- ◆ Have a basic introduction to various ways of building a website
- ◆ Know the factors to consider before you start building your website using a particular tool
- ◆ Understand these concepts easily with the example of sandwiches
- ◆ Explore WordPress and understand what makes it so popular
- ◆ Learn about a few major companies that have leveraged the power of WordPress to build their websites

Multiple road - One destination

Building a website is an art. But not all artists use the same tools. For example, consider the case of painters. Some painters may paint using watercolors, whereas some may just do pencil sketches. You can see various tools that a painter can use for making a painting in the following *Figure 1.2*:

Figure 1.2: Different tools for painting

And how can we forget the digital painters who can paint only on their iPads or other digital pads? But is the choice of tool a parameter for how good an artist they are? Absolutely No!

What matters is the painting they make in the end. That is the end product, and the skill or choice of the tool was just a means to reach it.

As painters can use different tools to create a painting, a web developer too has many options to choose from. The option that a web developer chooses depends on a lot of factors:

- Skillset and experience
- Kind of website they are building
- Speed of development

Many more factors come into the picture when we build complex websites such as the efficiency of the language/system we choose, how it has performed in speed tests, how many users it can handle, and so on. But to keep our discussion simple, we will only focus on the previously mentioned main points.

Skillset and experience

There are a variety of web developers around the world; some work on languages and some with libraries or frameworks. For example, these days, many frontend developers find themselves comfortable working with a popular library called ReactJS.

Enough with the complicated jargon. The point is that as you progress in the field of web development and gain more experience, your skillset will keep improving. In addition, you will pursue more flexibility for doing things your way, which will make you adopt newer tools.

So, with more knowledge and tools at your disposal, you will explore different ways to create a website.

Kind of Websites they are building

Not every type of painting requires the same tools. For example, some paintings can be made better with a pencil, whereas some can be executed better on an iPad or a digital pad, as shown in *Figure 1.3*:

Figure 1.3: An artist painting on a digital pad

Similarly, not all websites can be built in a better way using the same tools. Although it may be better to use simple website builders to build a one-page website for our personal website, the same may not be a great choice for a complicated website such as Facebook.

Speed of development

Speed of development required is a big parameter that developers have to consider before choosing the perfect tool for a job. Sometimes, due to the nature of the business or the urgency of the request, we may have to build a website really fast. So making everything from scratch might not be a good idea.

In such cases, even seasoned developers and big companies may use WordPress for building a website. It works great even for big companies and also helps them build websites fast.

Later in this chapter, we will let you know about a few large-scale professional websites, which are based on WordPress.

Let's eat Sandwiches

Earlier in this chapter, we were talking about different ways of building a website. So let's explore that further with the help of sandwiches. And if you feel like grabbing one before we proceed further, feel free to do that!

Figure 1.4: Ready to eat sandwiches made with fresh ingredients

When you want to eat a sandwich, there are various ways to do that. The easiest one is to order a readymade sandwich directly from a store or from your food delivery app.

But what if you don't like a particular ingredient added in the readymade sandwich, or what if you don't like the bread they use? Well, you can buy all the raw ingredients, make bread from flour directly at your home, and add only those ingredients in your sandwich that you really like.

Although the preceding option will surely give you a sandwich with your loved ingredients, isn't it too complicated? Isn't the effort involved more than the reward you get?

So, let's chuck that idea out and look at another way of getting the perfect sandwich. Let's walk in together at a Subway outlet.

Subway Sandwiches, for the sandwiches of your choice

Subway allows you to buy the sandwich of your choice, without you having to make everything from scratch. Depending on how hungry you are, you can even select the size of the bread – 6 inches or a foot long.

You can choose the type of bread you want for your sandwiches from their various options, such as Italian bread or honey oat bread. Then, depending on whether you are vegetarian or non-vegetarian, you can choose the base for your sandwich and then the add-ons or toppings that you want inside it, along with the sauces of your choice. So, there you go, a complete customized sandwich is ready for you without making it from scratch.

Although Subway can at almost all times match the exact choice of most of the customers, is that true for 100% of them? I have a friend who likes to have mashed half-boiled eggs in his sandwiches, and as far as I know, Subway doesn't have that! So, even if Subway can address the needs of most of the customers, there will still be a few who because of their super customized taste, they will have to make their own sandwiches.

To summarize, from the preceding example, there are three ways to make a sandwich:

- Order a complete readymade sandwich – a very easy process.
- Make everything from scratch – a very hard process.

- Get a customized sandwich from Subway, which would be exactly of choice for most of the customers – an easy process and almost fully customized too.

Now, let's understand how each sandwich type can be compared to the various options available for building a website.

Readymade Sandwiches

Just like ordering readymade sandwiches, there is an easy way of creating a website too. There are many readymade tools today, which can make the entire process of building a website very easy. But there is only so much you can do with these tools.

Generally, such websites are suitable for single-use cases only and you can't customize them as per your requirements. There are many options coming up for building websites this way such as Carrd, or even the very popular Wix, which would also fall in this bucket because it provides customization options; but it is not as much as WordPress (not even close to it).

Carrd, for example, only provides you with the option to create single landing page websites with few available templates. So, let's say you create a personal website there, and in the future, you want to sell one of your drawings via your website, you may not be able to do that.

Even your profile on websites like Medium or Facebook would fall in this category. Your profile link on these websites is also yours, as it identifies you and shows data that you have inputted. It is a small part of the Internet that belongs to you. You can have a Facebook page where you can showcase your products, or if you are a photographer, you can have an Instagram profile where you put up your pictures.

Isn't it really easy to do so? Just a few clicks, and you are ready to go, but then there are so many restrictions. For example, you can't add the link from where someone might be able to purchase your photograph on your Instagram post.

That is the limitation of these readymade sandwiches like website builders. They are very easy to set up with almost no specific knowledge required, but you will find yourself in a tight spot whenever you need any customization.

Making everything from Scratch, completely customized Sandwiches

Remember the example of my friend who likes having mashed half-boiled eggs in his sandwiches? For people like him, the best way may be to create a completely customized sandwich at home as the chef making his sandwich in the following *Figure 1.5*:

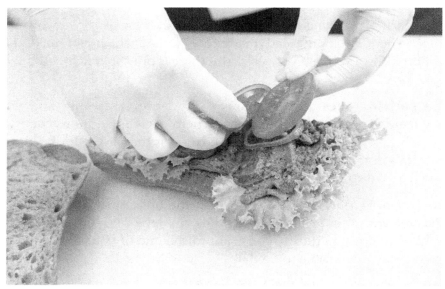

Figure 1.5: A chef making a sandwich

Drawing a parallel from this example, imagine you are the owner of YouTube. On surveying the consumers, one day your team decides to launch a new feature on the website which will help website visitors do live chat in live stream video. Now, this is a highly specialized feature, and in all probability, may never have been built before. However, websites and businesses like these create many such features, which is generally a first for consumers like us.

In such cases, their team has no option but to go to the whiteboard and build everything from scratch. This typically happens by using a combination of various techniques that involve:

♦ Setting up the right server infrastructure

♦ Choosing the right frontend library/framework

♦ Choosing the right backend language/framework

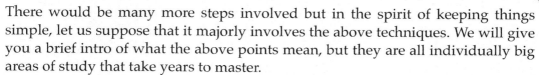

There would be many more steps involved but in the spirit of keeping things simple, let us suppose that it majorly involves the above techniques. We will give you a brief intro of what the above points mean, but they are all individually big areas of study that take years to master.

Servers

Servers is the place where a website is hosted or kept. Whenever you open a website in your browser, your browser downloads that webpage on your device and then opens it for you. For example, imagine a PDF file on your laptop, and if you want to send that PDF file to your friend, you will transfer it to a pen drive and then give the pen drive to your friend. He can then transfer the file to his/her device from there.

But what if you want to send it to your whole class? Giving out pen drives individually to each student in your class would be a tiresome job. So, probably you mail it out to everyone or share a Google Drive link for the file.

When you add your file on Google Drive, the file is stored somewhere on a server connected with the Internet, which allows your friends to connect to it and download the file to their device.

The same thing happens with a website. The only thing is that with the URL of your website, anyone in the world can connect to your server and download the webpage to their device via their browser and see your website. Isn't that fascinating?

Frontend

If you are tech savvy or have attended web development sessions in your school, you must have heard this term called "*HTML*".

Let's forget the term for now and first consider an example:

If anyone in the world has your home address, they can come and visit you at your home (obviously with your permission, though!). Your home address, in this case, becomes your URL, and your home is your server where you reside. If anybody has the address, they can come and fetch you from there.

How you look when someone comes to your home depends on what you are wearing that day! And also, on what your height is, the shape of your face, and so on. Your body, along with the clothes you wear, is your frontend. So that is what people see.

In the case of websites too, the webpage that you see in your browser is the frontend. The different boxes of content or headings that you see are defined with HTML, just like the shape of your face and height. And as you can make yourself look better by wearing good clothes, you can make different HTML sections look better with CSS.

HTML is the building block of a webpage that loads on your device, whereas CSS makes those building blocks look good. HTML stands for Hyper Text Markup Language and CSS stands for Cascading Style Sheet.

These days, many advanced frontend libraries/frameworks are also available to make frontend development easier and better. But we will keep that topic for another day!

Backend

We forgot to mention one crucial thing in the preceding example. Your body may decide your appearance, and you may make it look better with your clothes, but it is your mind that fundamentally defines you. That is what tells you what to speak and how to react.

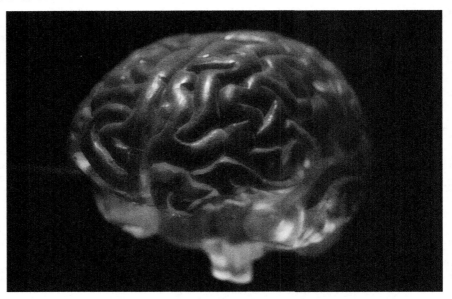

Figure 1.6: *A representation of the human brain*

Similarly, in the case of websites, even though the design of what you see is taken care of by frontend technologies, it is the backend that fills in data in those building blocks.

For example, open a YouTube website on one device, sign in with your account, and open your parent's YouTube account on another device, and ask them to login with their account. Notice the content on both devices.

The design of the website in both devices will look identically similar. However, the data or the suggestion for video in both devices will be completely different. The backend does this logic for sending different content as per different accounts, even though the frontend design remains the same.

Just for your knowledge, examples of popular backend languages used by companies these days are PHP, Java, NodeJS, Golang, and so on.

As with the frontend, there are many backend frameworks available such as Laravel, Spring Boot, and so on, but we won't be covering them in this book.

Subways Sandwiches and WordPress

Now, we come back to our customized sandwiches from Subway. As my friend had a unique taste, he had to make his sandwich on his own, but for most of the customers, they will be able to get the sandwich of their choice from Subway like the one shown in the following *Figure 1.7*:

Figure 1.7: A Subway like sandwich

Similarly, in the case of websites, very few big companies would want to build everything from scratch because they are building something that probably was never built before. And some people who just want a simple page would go for readymade website builders that we discussed earlier.

But the majority of website builders would want the process of building a website simple and also be able to tweak or change it as per their requirements.

Just like our Subway sandwiches, you don't have to make it completely on your own, but you can still get it as per your taste.

Welcome to the world of WordPress!

What is WordPress?

WordPress is a tool or system that allows you to build your website without writing a single piece of code but still gives you the power to change your website according to your requirements. And if you do want to code, there is also an option to get your hands dirty and code it on top of the WordPress system.

Figure 1.8: WordPress written on a paper

Tools or systems like WordPress fall into the category of **Content Management System (CMS)**. CMS helps you manage content on your website. You can use it to create new content or modify existing ones. Good CMS systems allow you to fully control the look and feel of your content as well, and help you to build a full-fledged website without writing a single piece of code!

Although you would have guessed it, let's just say it for the record! WordPress is the world's most popular CMS system. And here is a fun fact: more than 41% of the top 10 million websites in the world have been built using WordPress.

That number is huge!

There are hundreds and thousands of options available today for building websites. But the fact that more than 41% of top websites in the world have opted to use WordPress speaks of its power and usability.

WordPress was created by two genius developers – *Matt Mullenweg* and *Mike Little*. The first version of WordPress was released in 2003. And it has come a long way since then.

Originally, WordPress was used to create and manage blog websites. But now, it has become so advanced and multi-purpose that it is used to create online e-commerce websites, forums, membership sites, social networks, business websites, and more!

Who Uses It?

Anyone can use WordPress. After completing this book, you too would be equipped with the knowledge of wielding the powers of WordPress. And as discussed earlier, you can create any type of website you can dream of using this amazing tool.

Although we did mention earlier that more than 41% of the top websites in the world use WordPress, it can only help to look at some of the big names that use it.

The following are the five popular WordPress-based websites that you may have heard of:

1. **Microsoft News:**

    Yes, even the tech giants like Microsoft rely on WordPress to power their websites. For example, the blog or news section of Microsoft is based on WordPress, as shown here:

Figure 1.9: Screenshot of Microsoft News website

2. **PlayStation:**

    Do you love playing games on your PS? If so, you ought to love WordPress too! The blog of PlayStation that provides updates and news about all your favorite games is based on WordPress. Refer to *Figure 1.10*:

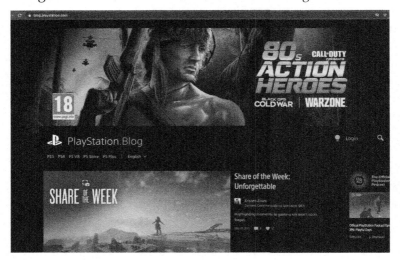

Figure 1.10: *Screenshot of PlayStation Blog*

3. **The Walt Disney:**

    The creator of your favorite cartoons also uses the popular CMS system – WordPress to manage its website.

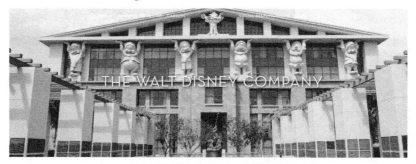

Figure 1.11: *Screenshot of The Walt Disney website*

4. **Angry Birds:**

Ever played this popular game? The website of Angry Birds is powered by our very beloved WordPress.

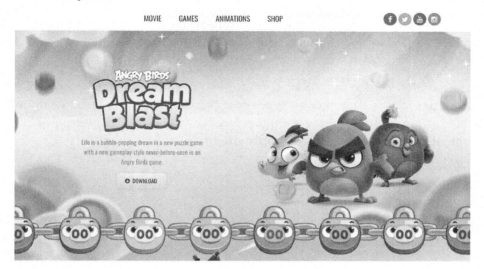

Figure 1.12: Screenshot of Angry Birds website

5. **Sony Music:**

The popular Sony company also uses WordPress to run its music website.

Figure 1.13: Screenshot of Sony Music website

The previously mentioned companies are only a few of a number of businesses that use WordPress to create a great website. These websites have an incredible number of visitors coming to their site on a daily basis. So, if they have chosen WordPress as their choice of technology, it must really be something.

And if these people can create such stunning websites using WordPress, then so can you! It might sound unbelievable now, but hey, we are just starting on our journey of learning WordPress.

By the end of this book, you will be confident enough to take these companies head on with your website that may even surpass them. Who knows? As we mentioned at the beginning of this chapter, a child is freer than a King. And with this freedom comes creativity that we adults can only dream of!

Recap

In this chapter, we covered a few cases that you as a website developer will have to consider before you start building a website. We also understood different ways to make a website and why WordPress is such a popular choice.

We ended the chapter by seeing how even major companies use WordPress to build their website. In the next chapter, we will start to set up our account on WordPress and take a step forward in our journey to become a WordPress expert.

Points to Remember

- There are various ways to build a website. Most businesses often consider their skillset, the kind of website they build, and the speed of development required before finalizing a technology.

- With readymade website builders, you can make your website easily but won't be able to make any changes.

- When you build a feature that hasn't been created before, you will have to make everything from scratch.

- Servers are the place where your website is hosted or kept.

- The frontend is the part of the website that defines how it will look in the user's browser.

- The backend is responsible for sending data that is to be shown in the frontend of the user.

- WordPress provides the best of both worlds. It allows you to build a website without writing a single line of code, but at the same time also allows you to do your customizations.

- A total of 41% of top websites in the world are made using WordPress. There are many big businesses too that use WordPress.

Multiple Choice Questions

1. Which one of these does business not consider while finalizing the technology they want to use to build the website?

   a. Their skillset

   b. Kind of website they are building

   c. Speed of development

   d. None of these

2. When shouldn't you use readymade website builders?

   a. When you want to build it fast

   b. When you want to make changes to it

   c. When you are looking for a simple way to build a website

   d. None of these

3. The server is responsible for:

   a. Defining how your website looks in the browser

   b. Writing logic for what data should be shown

   c. Hosting your website

   d. None of these

4. **Which one of these does WordPress not do?**

   a.   Help you build a website without writing code

   b.   Force you to use only one fixed design

   c.   Allow you to make changes to the website

   d.   All of these

Answer Key

1. d   2. b   3. c   4. b

Take it Further

o   Google and read about more companies that use WordPress to run their websites.

Chapter
2

Getting Started – Create Your Account and Start Exploring

Structure Bot

In this chapter, we will discuss the following topics:

- Signing up on WordPress
- Creating a free account
- Initial configuration of your website
- Exploring the dashboard

ow that we understand what WordPress is and why we should use it, it is time to start building websites on it. The first pre-requisite to do so is to create an account on WordPress.com. In this chapter, we will learn how to create an account on WordPress and get started with the process of building websites.

Objective Bot

At the end of this chapter, you will be able to:

- Set up your account on WordPress
- Create a default working website with access to a dashboard to make changes to it

Signing Up on WordPress

The signing up process on WordPress is really simple. If you have signed up on other websites like Facebook or Twitter, then you may find the process here to be familiar. You have to mention your personal details on these websites to set up your account. Similarly, you need to enter the details of your website and a few basic information about yourself to create an account on WordPress.

For all tutorials in this book, we suggest you to use a laptop with a Google Chrome browser. Most of the steps in the book can be followed on mobile devices or any other devices and browsers. However, it is recommended to use a laptop because you are still new to building websites using WordPress. And a laptop will give you a broader view with more options.

And we suggest using Google Chrome because there can be a difference in how different browsers react to different settings, themes, plugins, and so on (which we will discuss in the upcoming chapters). We have tested the tutorials in this book on the Google Chrome browser and hence would recommend you to use the same.

To start the signing up process, you will have to visit https://wordpress.com/ on your device. The page that would open up will look somewhat like the following screenshot:

The screenshots added in this book are from the time the book was written or last updated. There can be few design changes during the time you read it, but at an overall level, the options would remain the same.

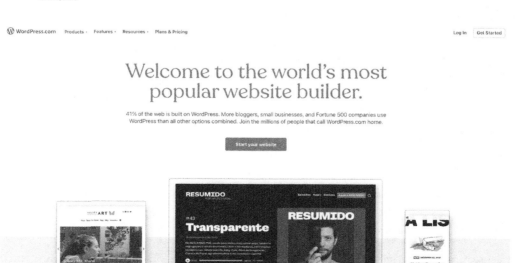

Figure 2.1: WordPress homepage

This type of homepage of such websites is technically called a Landing Page. As the name suggests, the Landing page is the page where a website visitor first lands. It serves as an entry point for the whole website. A website visitor who is completely new to WordPress will always first land on this page to get an idea of what it is about and then move on to other pages.

Feel free to take your time to explore this page. WordPress explains how it helps you to create a beautiful and professional website on its landing page. You can scroll to the bottom of the page and see what WordPress has to say about itself. Once you are done exploring, come back to the top of this page and click on the "Start your website" button in the middle of the screen or the "Get Started" button on the top right. Both the buttons will take you to the same page, so you can click either of them.

The buttons like "Start your website" and "Get Started" are called as CTA buttons. CTA stands for Call-to-action buttons. These are the buttons that motivate your website visitors to take certain actions on your website. They motivate them to move forward and explore your website further, in the direction that you want them to take.

After clicking one of those buttons, you will land on the registration page, which would look like the following screenshot:

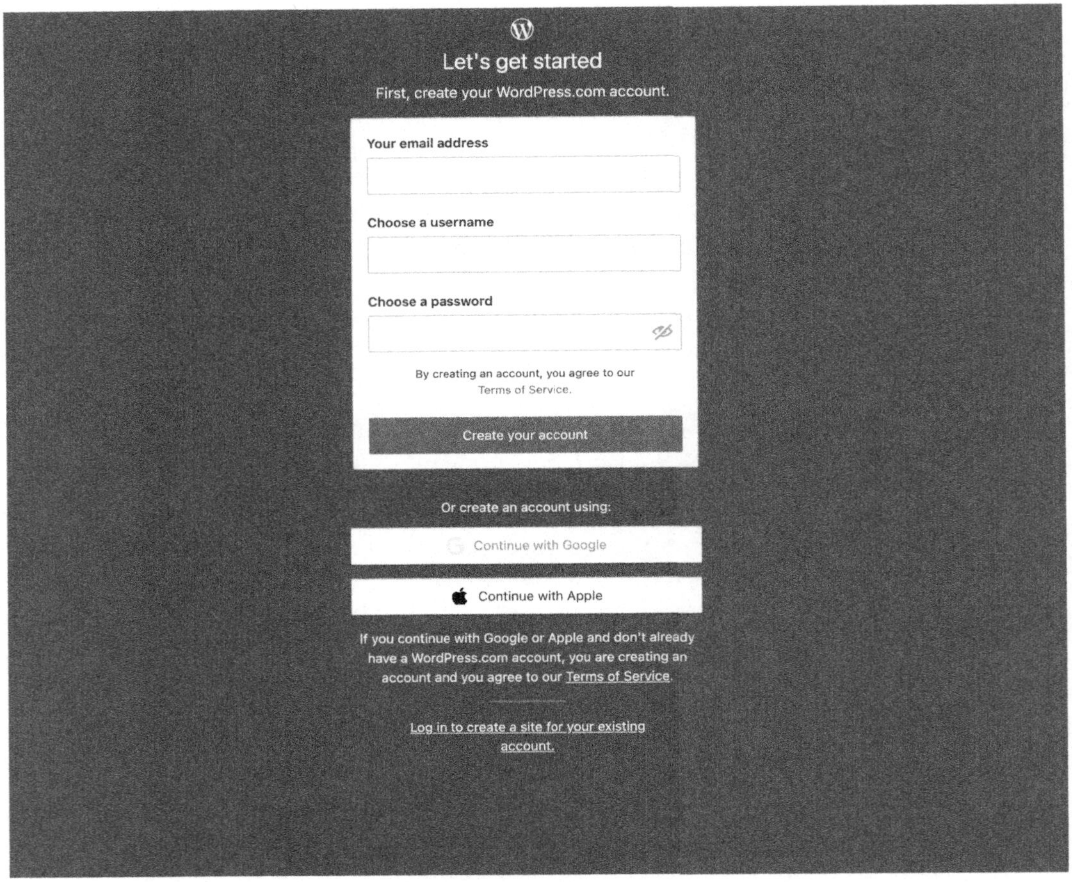

Figure 2.2: First step of WordPress registration

This registration page is one of the 3 steps you have to complete to create an account on WordPress. There are various ways available to complete this step:

1. You can enter your email address, add a username and password, and move ahead.

2. Complete these steps by connecting your Google account with WordPress.

3. Complete these steps by connecting your Apple account with WordPress.

We will use the first way to complete this registration process.

Creating your domain

Go ahead and please enter your email address in the first input box, as shown in *figure 2.2*. This email address will be linked to your WordPress account. Therefore, add the one which you want to use to create the website.

Next, we have to select a username. The username needs to be unique and would be the unique identifier of your WordPress account. You can use this username later to login to your WordPress account.

Your username can be any alphanumeric word as long as no one has used it. There are a few restrictions, though. For example, you cannot use special characters like '@ _ / *' in the username, and only small case letters are allowed along with numbers.

You can now go ahead and try different usernames. In case, the username you enter is not unique, WordPress will let you know that with a red text below the box. In that case, you can enter a different username. This is just like creating your email ids. If you have created an email id yourself before, then you know that it has to be completely unique. Similarly, you need to come up with a unique username for your WordPress account.

Once you have come up with an acceptable username, you can then enter your password. Make sure you choose a strong password (but also that you can remember).

After entering the password, click on the "**Create your account**" button.

Selecting a domain

In the first step, you entered your basic details, which you will use later to login to your WordPress account. In the second step, you will provide a few details about the website you will build.

Figure 2.3: Second step of registration

The first sentence on this page says, "Let's get your site a domain". So, what is this domain? The literal meaning of the word domain is the area or territory that is owned by a particular entity. In the case of internet websites too, it is almost the same. Your domain is the part of internet that is owned by you. It is the named web address of your website. For example, facebook.com is the domain of Facebook and it is owned by its company. Similarly, for Twitter, its domain is twitter.com and Instagram.com for Instagram.

At this step, WordPress wants to know which domain you want for your website. Please note, just like with username in the last step, you cannot buy any domain you want. If you want to buy facebook.com, you cannot do that because it has already been purchased by Facebook. Your domain needs to be something that hasn't been purchased by someone else before. So, go ahead and type the domain you want in the box shown in the picture and see if it is available.

After you type the domain name in the box, you will get a few suggestions, as shown in the following screenshot:

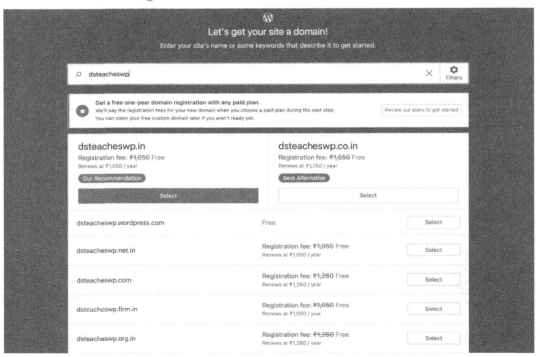

Figure 2.4: Selecting a domain on WordPress

I have entered my domain as dsteacheswp (WP is often used as a short form for WordPress). You can see there are various suggestions coming up. Let's consider the first three suggestions: dsteacheswp.in, dsteacheswp.co.in, and dsteacheswp.wordpress.com.

On the internet, there are different kinds of extensions available for a website. So, what do extensions mean? Extensions are generally the last part of your web URL. The most popular extension obviously is "com". Com is probably the most unrestricted extension used by most of the organizations and individuals across the world.

These extensions have some meaning attached to them as well. For example, the extension "in" in the preceding screenshot identifies your website as being focused on Indian users. A website with extension "edu" would mean that your website represents an educational entity.

But if you decide to buy your own domain, it will cost you. Even though .in and .co.in domains in the preceding screenshot show their price as free, you will still have to purchase a paid package from WordPress. And at this stage, we don't want to make a payment. We will come back to paid options in *Chapter 13, Going for a Paid Plan – Is It Required?*

Companies like WordPress that also sell domains are called Domain Registrars. There are many domain registrars. The entity which controls all these domain registrars is called ICANN (Internet Corporation for Assigned Names and Numbers). It is in a way a central place for all domain names, and is often also referred to as the "phonebook of internet".

Let's explore the third suggestion now – dsteacheswp.wordpress.com. This is a subdomain of the WordPress website itself. What is a subdomain?

Let's suppose you have a house with many rooms. If you own the house, you can invite your friends and give them a room of their own in your house. It won't cost your friend anything because he is taking a room in your house and you are not charging him/her for that. But if your friend decides to buy a house of his own,

then definitely it will not come for free. They will have to pay to buy the whole house to whosoever they are buying it from.

Similarly, once you buy a domain, you own it. The domain becomes like a house. You can partition this house and make multiple rooms, which would be subdomains in this case. And because you own the domain, you don't have to pay anything when you are giving away a subdomain of the main website to someone else. So, a subdomain is a type of domain that is a part of another domain. In the preceding suggestion, dsteacheswp.wordpress.com is a domain that is a part of the main domain wordpress.com.

WordPress acts as you did for your friend in the preceding example. It provides this benefit to you to create a free domain using its subdomain. So, we will go ahead with this option. For the domain that you entered in the preceding box, click "Select" on its ".wordpress.com" version.

Choosing a plan

After clicking on select, you will be taken to the final page of registration, where you will be asked to select a paid package. Again, the step will have different plans, as shown in the following screenshot:

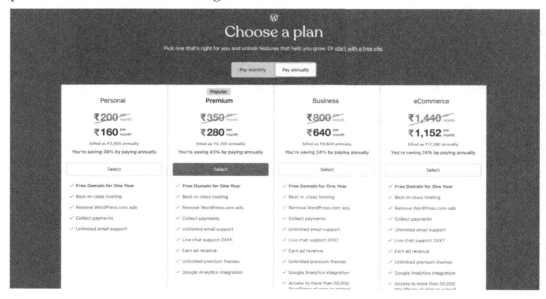

Figure 2.5: Final step of account creation on WordPress

As we previously mentioned, we will cover premium-paid options in *Chapter 13, Going for a Paid Plan - Is It Required?* So, we will skip this step. To skip this step, simply click on the text "start with a free site" in the following sentence with "Choose a plan" heading.

After you click that, WordPress will take a minute to prepare your site and send you to your dashboard. Do not close this tab, and we will come back to this dashboard later in this chapter.

An additional step

After completing the registration steps, check your email once. WordPress must have sent an email to you to verify your email address. WordPress needs to know if the email you mentioned during registration was a valid email address or not. To do so, it does this verification. Your account will be activated only when you confirm and verify your email address.

You simply need to open the email from WordPress for this. The email would have a subject like "Activate dsteacheswp" (your website name will be present in your case) or "Confirm your email address". Open that email, and there will be a button that you will have to click. Click that button and wait for the web page to load. You will get a small prompt that your email has now been confirmed.

After you complete the above steps, go ahead and then open your website in a new tab (but in the same window where you are signed in the WordPress dashboard). For example, my website URL is dsteacheswp.wordpress.com, and yours would be similar to the name you chose. Voila!! You can now see your website up and running. Ours looks like the following screenshot:

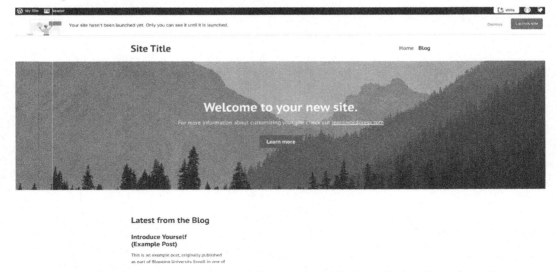

Figure 2.6: Website preview with default settings after completing the registration

Please note that only you can see this website for now when you are logged in to your dashboard as we haven't yet launched this website. The website is present there with a default setting. If someone tries to open this website, who isn't logged in to the dashboard, they will see a Coming Soon page as shown in the following screenshot:

Figure 2.7: Coming soon page shown to users who are not logged into the site dashboard

In the upcoming chapters, we will explore how to change every aspect of our website and make it ready for launch.

Exploring the dashboard

In the preceding steps, when WordPress had prepared your site, it would have taken you to your site dashboard. Also, when you would have confirmed your email, you would have landed on your site dashboard.

In case you accidentally closed the dashboard, you can open wordpress.com again, and WordPress will automatically take you to your dashboard because you are still signed in. If you have been logged out, you can just login again using the login button, enter your credentials, and then you will be taken to your dashboard.

Your site dashboard would look somewhat like this:

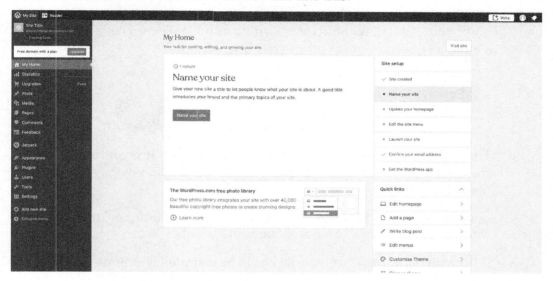

Figure 2.8: WordPress dashboard

You can see so many options on the dashboard here. WordPress has even listed down the steps you can follow to set up your site. We will follow some of these steps and more in the next chapter to start the process of making our site ready for launch.

You can explore the various options in the menu on the dashboard. You can also open those pages and see what those options provide. We will cover all the essential options in the upcoming chapters in detail.

We covered all the essential steps to get started with WordPress in this chapter. We created our account, chose a domain name, browsed through the premium plans, and finally landed on our dashboard. We can also see how our default website now looks, and it opens up with our URL!

In the next chapters, we will change every bit of the default website, so that it serves our use case. After that, we will transform it completely into whatever we want our website to be.

And that is the power of WordPress. In just a few clicks, we have a working website ready, and at the same time, we have the power to customize it completely. All that without even writing a single piece of code. The journey to build a super amazing website has just started!

Points to Remember

- The sign-up process on WordPress is very simple. It is almost as easy as signing up on Facebook or other websites. Make sure you have an email id ready for signing up.

- Your username on WordPress has to be completely unique. Your username can contain only small case alphabets and numbers.

- A domain name for your website has to be completely unique in the world.

- Extension of a website is typically its last part after the dot. The most popular extension in the world is ".com". Different extensions can mean various things

- Subdomains are a part of another domain.

- Choosing a subdomain of wordpress.com is completely free on WordPress. For choosing a domain, we will have to buy a premium paid package.

- You need to confirm your email id after completing all the registration steps to confirm and activate your account.

- After completing all the registration steps, you can open your website with the domain you chose.

- Only users who are logged in to the dashboard can open the website until it is published and launched. Other users will see "Coming Soon", if they try to open your website.

Multiple Choice Questions

1. Username on WordPress cannot contain:

   a. Small case letters such as a,b,c…

   b. Upper case letters such as A,B,C…

c.   Numbers such as 1,2,3...

    d.   None of these

2.   Two websites can have the same URL:

    a.   True

    b.   False

3.   Which one of these domains can you register for free on WordPress?

    a.   Letslearnwordpress.com

    b.   Letslearnwordpress.co.in

    c.   Letslearnwordpress.wordpress.com

    d.   Letslearnwordpress.edu

4.   Once the site is prepared but not launched, which one of these will be able to see the site?

    a.   Any logged in wordpress.com user

    b.   Only those wordpress.com users who have access to your site dashboard and are logged in

    c.   Anyone on internet

    d.   None of these

Answer Key

   1. b   2. b   3. c   4. b

Take it Further

o   Explore the options on the dashboard and familiarize yourself with different WordPress jargons.

o   Google and read more about the role of ICANN.

Setting Up Your Site

In this chapter, we will discuss the following topics:

- ◆ Setting up website branding
- ◆ Exploring user management on WordPress
- ◆ Checking website activity
- ◆ Analyzing website statistics

So far, we have understood what WordPress is and how to create our account there. Now, we will set up the website that we created in the previous chapter. This is a crucial phase in building the website because you will decide your website's name, tagline, and more. So, now would be a good time to give some more thought about how the website would be.

Any website that is created goes through this phase where the website creator brainstorms about it, thinks about the team that will make it, and then formulates a way to launch it.

At the end of this chapter, you will:

- ◆ Know the basic steps of setting up your website on WordPress
- ◆ Start adding branding for your website, such as its name, tagline, and logo
- ◆ Be able to take help from your friends by forming a team to build your website
- ◆ Be able to track all activities on your website at once and see the number of visitors coming to your website

Setting up website branding

Before setting up the branding of our website, it is important to understand what branding really means. Branding is the process of adding meaning to a particular product or a company as a whole.

Let us understand this with an example. Apple is a renowned brand in the world. What does Apple do, though? It is a company that makes phones, laptops, and other electronic items, as shown in the following screenshot (refer to *Figure 3.1*). For example, consider Apple phones. But Apple isn't the only company that makes phones. There are many more such brands in the world.

Figure 3.1: Few Apple products

Yet, people consider Apple's phones to be unique and different from others. They don't just call it a phone; they call it an iPhone. That is the power of branding. It helps a brand to differentiate itself in the minds of customers even though it does the same thing. Branding adds a specific meaning to your product that makes it different from other company's products.

It takes time for such powerful branding to build up and is done via different methods like good marketing, building a great product, and more. But the starting point for any branding activity is its name, tagline, and logo. That is what defines your website and brand the first time someone sees it, although there is a lot more to do for branding as you grow your website.

WordPress allows you to add a site logo, name, and tagline. So, let's add that. In the left sidebar menu, hover over **Settings**, and then click on **General**. The **"General"** option will come up as highlighted in a red box as shown in *Figure 3.2*:

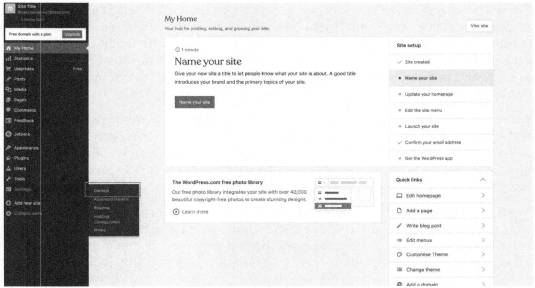

Figure 3.2: *General settings option in the sidebar menu*

The general settings page will have many options, as shown in the following screenshot:

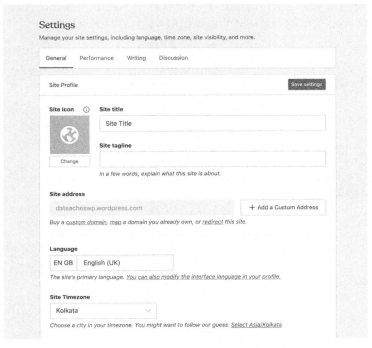

Figure 3.3: *General settings page*

We will concern ourselves with only 3 settings here, that is **Site Icon**, **Site title,** and **Site tagline**. If you have decided on the title of your site, enter it in the **Site title** box. Please note that the site title need not be the same as your website URL name. It can be more descriptive or slightly different if you want it to be. Many people tend to keep their site title the same as the domain name as it becomes easier for the customers to remember the website URL.

We will go ahead with the same name as the domain name, which is DS Teaches WP, but obviously with proper spacing and upper case wherever required. You can also go ahead with the same name or change it to what you want. Also, do note that if you are not sure of the site title, you can add any site title for now, and you can change it later as well by coming back to this page.

Next, let's enter a tagline for our website. A tagline is a short, catchy description of your product, which communicates about your brand or website. It is suggested to keep it short to about 5–7 words and not make it very long. For example, the tagline we are setting for our website is *"Learn WordPress with ease"*. This is because we are trying to communicate to our visitors that they can learn WordPress easily via our website. You can select a similar tagline for your website, which serves this purpose.

Now, the third step of branding is to add the site icon. This site icon can be a logo for your website. If you don't have a logo ready, you can skip this step or just write the first alphabet of your website name in a big font in MS Word or Google Docs, take its screenshot, and add it here. It may not be a perfect logo but it will do for setting up our website. You can always update your logo later.

To add a **Site Icon**, click on the **Change** button. After clicking on the **Change** button, a box with images will appear, which is available in your WordPress account. The box will look as shown in the following *Figure 3.4*:

Figure 3.4: *Media upload box in WordPress*

We don't have our site icon in our WordPress account, so we will click on the **Add new** button and upload it from our laptop. After clicking on **Add new**, navigate to the folder where your site icon is located on your laptop, select it, and add it. Once it is added, as shown in the preceding box, make sure the new image is selected, and then click on **Continue**. You will then get an option to crop/edit this image that you have selected; however, you can skip this step if you do not want to modify your icon.

We have now added all the three things required to set up our initial branding of the website. So we will now go ahead and click on the **Save settings** button. Once the settings are saved, you will get a prompt saying "**Settings Saved Successfully.**"

Let us open the URL of our website now and see how it has changed. Here is how our website looks (refer to *Figure 3.5*):

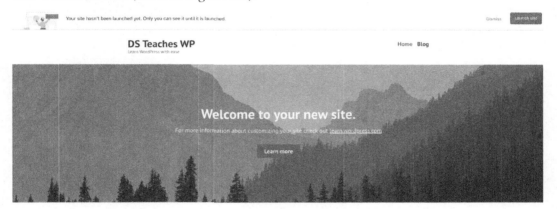

Figure 3.5: Updated site preview after setting up branding

Note the change in site title and site tagline. If you have also added a Site Icon, note the image and text in the tab heading in Google Chrome. The tab heading is the place where you close a tab. The site title would come there just before the cross button, and the Site Icon will be shown before the Site title.

Exploring user management on WordPress

Why does Google have so many employees? There are thousands of people at Google working on its website. Why?

A website is a complex thing. There are many things to do when you are building your website. We just covered the branding aspect of it, but there can be many other things like managing the products that are being sold on your website, writing articles to provide knowledge to your visitors, and more!

During the start, you can do most of these things on your own, but as your website grows bigger, you may want to create a team to manage it. And this is where *user management* on WordPress comes into the picture.

You can add different users with different permission levels to your WordPress account. We will cover permission levels (roles) in detail shortly. The users that you add to your WordPress account will be able to access your dashboard.

Adding a new user

Let's add a new user to our WordPress account. On the left sidebar menu, hover over users, and then click on the **Add New** button. A page to add users will open, as shown in the following screenshot:

← Back   Invite People

Usernames or emails

Enter up to 10 WordPress.com usernames or email addresses at a time.

Role

○ Administrator
    Full power over the site: can invite people, modify the site settings, etc.

○ Editor
    Has access to all posts and pages.

○ Author
    Can write, upload photos to, edit, and publish their own posts.

○ Contributor
    Can write and edit their own posts but can't publish them.

◉ Follower
    Can read and comment on posts and pages.

Learn more about roles

Custom message

500 characters remaining

(Optional) Enter a custom message to be sent with your invitation.

Send invitation

Figure 3.6: Add user page

To add a new user who may be your friend, enter their username or email address in the first box. You can enter up to 10 people's email addresses at once by pressing *Enter* and keep on adding. But we will only add one as this is the first time we are adding a user.

The next option is to select the role, which will decide the user's permissions on your WordPress dashboard. There are 5 roles available:

◆ Administrator: Your current account has the administrator privilege, which means you can edit any aspect of your site, add new users, modify settings such as site title, and more! If you select the Administrator, then your friend will also get the same privilege. In case you are building this website with a partner, then giving him/her the administrator privilege too would be a good idea.

◆ Editor: An Editor only has access to add/change the posts and pages. We will cover posts and pages in detail in the upcoming chapters, but this essentially means that a person with this role can change the content that appears on the site, but not the site settings. They can also not add any user or change their role.

◆ Author: While an Editor can change the content in the post or the page created by any Author, the Author can change only the post that he/she has created. Let's understand this with an example. Say you have added two friends, one as the Author and one as the Editor. Then whenever your friend with the Author role adds the posts, he/she can only edit the post that they have created. An Author cannot edit the post of another Author. But an Editor can edit the post of any Author.

◆ Contributor: The Contributor and Author differ only in one aspect. While an Author can publish his/her post on your site directly, a Contributor can only add a post. He/she cannot publish it, and an Editor will have to publish that post for it to appear on your website.

◆ Follower: A Follower cannot do anything on your WordPress dashboard directly. He/she can only add comments on the post and pages of your WordPress website.

Note

An editor on WordPress is very similar to editors in book publishing companies. While an author may work only on his/her book, an editor would be working with multiple authors at once and editing all their books. An author won't be able to edit the book of another author. If you are still having difficulty understanding these roles, then you can read more about how authors and editors work in traditional publishing/ newspaper organizations.

You can select the role that you want to allocate to your friend based on the following description:

Once you add a user on WordPress, it automatically sends an email to the user informing that you have added them to their website. This is called an **invite**. If the person you have invited wants to work on your website, they will accept your invitation. Post acceptance, they will be asked to create a password for their account (in case they don't already have a WordPress account), and then they too would be able to access your dashboard after logging into WordPress. They will only see those options on WordPress, which they can access according to their role.

But, when you send an invite, your friend may not know exactly what it is about. So, in the last box, which is **Custom Message**, you can write a message in under 500 characters, which would be sent in the invite email. This would give your friend a context of what the invite is about. You can let them know about your website in the email and what you want them to do on your website.

Once you have filled these three fields, you can click on the **Send Invite** button, and the invitation will be sent. Congratulations! You have now created a team to work on your website. This is your first step to becoming the CEO of your own brand/website!

Checking website activity

As you add multiple users to your website, you may also want to check what they do on your website. Let's take an example to understand this.

Suppose you have 20 articles on your website, and one day you have an argument with one of your editors. In a rage, the editor goes ahead and deletes 10 articles on your website. This can affect your website greatly! But how would you confirm who did this among your editors so that you can take appropriate actions? You will need some kind of proof.

There is a feature on WordPress that does just this. It provides you details of what users are doing on your dashboard. It tracks every change on your website and tells you which user did what.

To check the Activity Log, hover over Jetpack on your sidebar menu and then click on the **Activity Log**. Here's what the page would look like (refer to *Figure 3.7*):

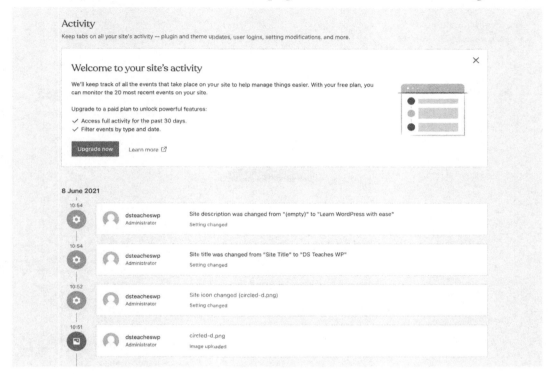

Figure 3.7: *Activity log of your WordPress site*

You can see exactly how WordPress shows details of every activity with date and time and who did it. The most recent update done by me here was updating the site description. As we are still on a free plan, we can only see 20 most recent activities on the site. We will later see how premium plans can help us get more past activity details in later chapters.

It is quite a useful tool, and you should check this on a daily basis to see what activities are being done on your website by your team.

Analyzing website statistics

While we are setting up our website, there is one crucial thing that we need to check. How will you know if your website is performing well? The parameter for

that would be how many people are visiting your website and if that number is increasing or not.

WordPress has a Statistics feature that provides you various useful statistics about your website. To access this feature, click on **Statistics** from the sidebar menu, and you will see a page as shown in the following screenshot:

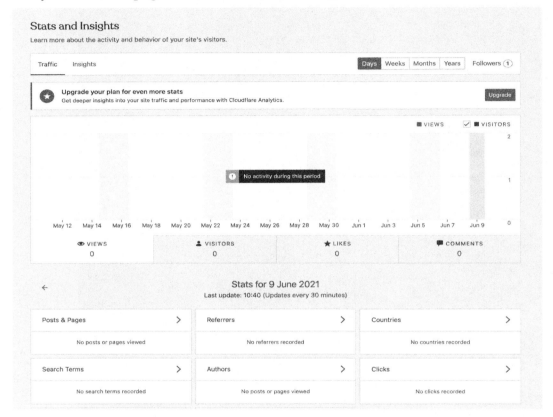

Figure 3.8: Traffic Statistics of your site

This page provides you the traffic details of your website. Traffic here basically means the information of visitors coming to your website. When there are many cars on the road, we say that there is a lot of traffic. Similarly, high-traffic websites have many visitors and low-traffic websites have fewer visitors.

It shows No activity in *Figure 3.8* because we haven't yet launched this website. Once we do that, you should return to this page every day and note how many visitors are coming to your website. You should keep track of it to see how your website is growing. There are different options like **Views**, **Visitors**, **Likes**, and **Comments** on this page. You can change these tabs and see what each one of them is showing. We will discuss some of these terms in the next chapter too.

Once you have data for your website, you can also see which post is performing the best or which author is having the best posts and which country is your website most popular in. All these data points will be shown in their respective boxes on this page.

We have one more tab next to **Traffic**, which is **Insights**. Let's click on it. A page like the one in *Figure 3.9* would open:

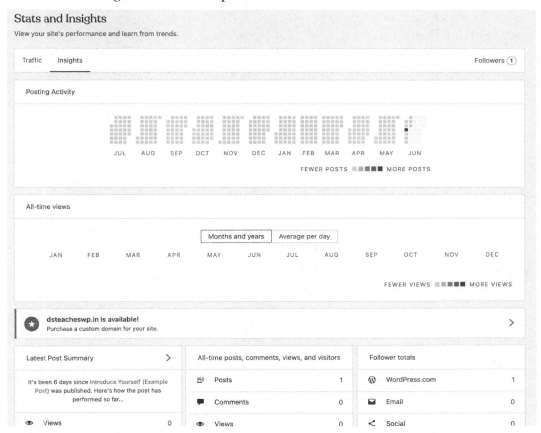

Figure 3.9: Insights about your website

Insights provide aggregate/summarized data about your website. For example, you can see how many posts are being published on your website and what the all-time views look like. WordPress uses a color-coding system to show this data on a calendar for the past 365 days from today. This kind of chart system is called a *"Calendar Chart"*.

The darker the color, the relatively higher the number on that day is. The lighter the color, the relatively lesser the number on that day is.

Recap

We have covered the process of setting up our website in this chapter. We did branding of our website, created a team, understood how to track the work of our team, and also check the statistics of the website once it is launched. Equipped with this knowledge, you are now ready to start working on your site. You should apply the things you have learned in this chapter before you start the next steps. It is always good to work in groups, and that is why your teachers also ask you to complete your tasks in groups very often. It makes the work interesting, teaches you about teamwork, and is also beneficial for creating a better result.

Let's end this chapter with an African saying:

"If you want to go fast, go alone. If you want to go far, go together."

In the next chapter, we will learn a few website terminologies that we will use extensively in this book and in our web development journey.

Points to Remember

- Branding is the process of adding meaning to a particular product or a company as a whole, which would differentiate your product (website) in the minds of your customer

- A tagline is a short, catchy description of your product, which communicates what your brand or website is about.

- There are five kinds of users that you can add to your website – Administrator, Editor, Author, Contributor, and Follower.

- Activity Log tracks every change on your website and tells you which user did what.

- The Traffic tab in Statistics provides you with data related to visitors coming to your website. You can also see that data on a daily basis.

- Insights tab in Statistics provides you aggregate/summarized data about your website on a Calendar Chart

Multiple Choice Questions

1. Which one of these is a part of setting up your website branding on WordPress?

    a. Site title

    b. Site description

    c. Site icon

    d. All of these

2. How many users can you add to your website at once in WordPress?

    a. 6

    b. 5

    c. 8

    d. 10

3. There can be only one Administrator on a WordPress website.

    a. True

    b. False

4. Which one of these does not have access to publish a post on WordPress?

    a. Administrator

    b. Contributor

    c. Author

    d. Editor

5. Calendar Chart shows data for past how many days from today?

    a. 30 days

    b. 90 days

    c. 365 days

    d. None of these

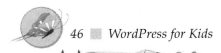

Answer Key

1. d   2. d

3. b   4. b

5. c

Take it Further

Google and read more about:

- o   Other kinds of branding are done by different websites. You can Google search "what kind of branding does a website do".

- o   Bar charts and calendar charts. The bar chart is used in the Traffic tab in the Statistics option of WordPress, whereas the calendar chart is used in the Insights tab. Learn more about how to read these charts.

Chapter 4

Few Website Terminologies

Structure Bot

In this chapter, we will discuss the following topics:

◆ Header and footer

◆ Menu

◆ Hyperlinks

◆ Responsive design

◆ Rich text editors

◆ Frontend and backend

When you play cricket, you often say *"Catch Out"* or *"LBW"* when a wicket goes off. But you don't explain what catch out or LBW essentially means. You have used these terms so often with your friends, that its meaning comes naturally to you. But, if we bring you a complete cricket newbie or if you are, then these terms may sound like an alien language to you.

The same happens with anything new you do. There are terms or terminologies in any area of study or even games, and someone who hasn't heard them before may not be aware of it. But these terms become a means of communication for people who have spent some time working in that field or playing that game.

As we are venturing into the world of web development, there are a few terminologies that you should also know about. In this chapter, we will cover few terms that we will often use throughout the book, and it would be repetitive to explain every time we use them.

Objective Bot

At the end of this chapter, you will:

◆ Be familiarized with a few basic terminologies of web development, which we will use throughout this book

◆ Be able to understand some of the key terms that web developers often use in their conversations

Earlier in *Chapter 1, WordPress and Subway – Understanding WordPress with the Help of Sandwiches*, we had used our body as an example to understand a few concepts related to web development. So let us use it again. The header and footer are both an extension of the word head and foot, which are parts of our body. The head is the part that is on top of our body, while our foot is the bottom-most part of our body.

By the analogy, the header is that part of the website, which comes the first, and the footer is that part of the website, which comes at last. So typically, we see menus coming in the header section of most websites, and we see the copyright text or few menu items along with contact form in the footer of most websites.

Both headers and footers are an important part of your website. The header is the first thing a visitor sees on your website, and the footer is the last. Therefore, it is a good idea to have important links to your website pages at these places so that your web visitor can easily navigate.

However, it is not mandatory for a website to have a header or footer. Some websites may remove them depending upon their design requirements.

Let us look at a few examples.

Here is the Google homepage (refer to *Figure 4.1*). The header has been highlighted in the red box in the screenshot, whereas the footer has been highlighted in the blue box.

Figure 4.1: *Google search homepage*

We can see both header and footer on the Google Search homepage. Let us now look at the Twitter homepage as shown in *Figure 4.2*:

Figure 4.2: *Twitter homepage for non-logged in users*

Here, you can see the footer highlighted in white. But apparently, there is no visible header on this page.

Feel free to visit more websites you frequently use and try to identify the header and footer on those websites.

Menu

We talked about the menu while discussing the header and footer too. Menus are typically a part of the header and footer in most websites.

A menu is a collection of links that point to major pages of your website. Let us take a look at the Amazon website to understand this:

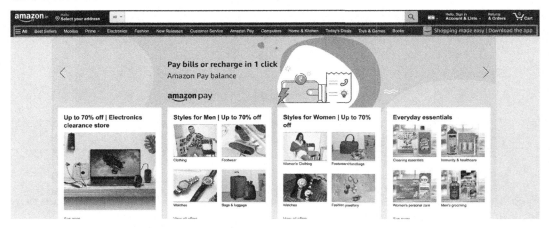

Figure 4.3: *Menu on Amazon homepage*

The menu in the preceding screenshot has been highlighted in the red box. For better clarity, you can also open the Amazon website on your laptop and check this out. Here, you can see how Amazon has mentioned the link to major pages such as the **Mobiles** page, the **Electronics** page, and more in this menu itself. This makes it easy for you to directly visit these pages on Amazon and buy the product you want.

Earlier, we mentioned that menus are typically a part of the header and footer in most websites. But that is not true at all times. Menus can be present at other places too. One of the other most common places for menus is the Sidebar. For example, in the same Amazon website, click the icon just before **All** (the one with three horizontal lines).

A sidebar menu will come up, which will look like the one in the following figure:

Figure 4.4: Sidebar menu on Amazon

As you can see here, the sidebar menu is neither a part of the header or footer. The purpose of the menu is to help your users reach the page that they want. And there are various ways in which a menu can do that.

Hyperlinks

This one is easy. If you have worked on MS Word or Google Docs, then you must have used this feature. When you select a group of words or a word and link it to a website link, it is called a **hyperlink**. Now, when the user clicks on that word, he/she will be taken to the link you added. Often, such terms that are hyperlinked are denoted by blue color and are underlined.

The word or group of words that you link to a website is called *"anchor text"*.

Responsive design

We have several devices with us nowadays, such as a laptop, tablet, and phone too! Some people even use huge TV screens for surfing the internet. So, a website that you create should open up properly on all of these devices. And that is easier said than done.

Web developers have to make a lot of considerations to ensure that their website opens up properly on all of these devices and its functionality adapts as per the screen size.

This kind of design that looks good on screens of all sizes is called **responsive design**. Why did you ask? Since the design is responsive to the size of the screen. That's quite an intuitive name in itself!

The idea is that a website should be like water. Water takes the shape of the container in which it is kept. If you add it to a glass, it takes the shape of a glass; if you add it to a bottle, it takes the shape of a bottle. Similarly, no matter where a person opens your website, it should adapt as per the screen size of the person.

Responsive design is a must for websites these days. Gone are the days when people only used laptops or computers for visiting websites. Instead, most of the websites today are visited majorly by mobile users. And therefore, responsive design has become increasingly important with each passing day.

Do you know what would happen in the case, let's say, your website looked good on laptop but not on mobile? Your business would lose customers and ultimately money if your website is for commercial purposes. Many businesses/companies throughout the world have suffered it.

While building our website, we will make sure that it is properly responsive so that we don't suffer this problem.

Rich text editors

Let us come back to the example of MS Word and Google Docs. When you are writing something in these two applications, there is a lot of formatting that you can do. For example, you can change the font size, line height, color of the text, and more!

Basically, on these applications too, you are writing text, and hence they too are text editors. But, since they also allow you to add a lot of formatting to your text, they are called **rich text editors**. WordPress also has rich text editors, as we will see in the upcoming chapters, allowing us to add formatting to the text on our website.

But here's a quick display of the rich text editor on WordPress, which is shown in *Figure 4.5*. Notice the formatting options available on the right side. We will cover them in detail later.

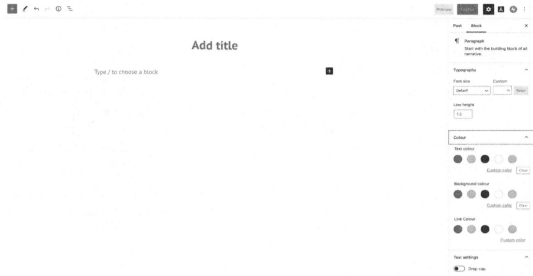

Figure 4.5: WordPress Post Editor

As you may have guessed, as rich text editors have formatting options, normal text editors do not have any formatting options available. An example would be the Notepad application in your Windows laptop.

Frontend and Backend

We have already covered frontend and backend in depth in *Chapter 1, WordPress and Subway – Understanding WordPress with the Help of Sandwiches*. If you want, you can go back and revise it once before we move ahead.

In WordPress websites, the website that you see when you type your domain name is your frontend, and the dashboard that we have been using so far can be called as its backend.

We will often refer to the frontend and backend for toggling between the website, which opens up when you directly type the domain name and dashboard.

We discussed a few key terminologies in this chapter, which we will use throughout the book. There are numerous other terms used in the world of web development, which you will come across as you explore further. However, acquaintance with the above terms is a good starting point for working on WordPress.

In the next chapter, we will learn about posts and pages, which are the building blocks of a WordPress website. They will help us add content to our website and engage our users.

- The header is often the first part of your website that is visible, whereas the footer is the last part of the website.

- It is not mandatory for a website to have a header and footer.

- A menu is a collection of links that point to major pages of your website.

- When you select a group of words or a word and link it to a website link, it is called a Hyperlink.

- The kind of design that looks good on screens of all sizes is called responsive design.

- Applications where you can write the text and that allow you to add formatting to it are called rich text editors.

- In the case of WordPress websites, the website that you see when you type your domain name is your frontend, and the dashboard that we have been using so far can be called as its backend.

Multiple Choice Questions

1. A website should mandatorily have:
   - *a.* Header
   - *b.* Footer
   - *c.* Hyperlink
   - *d.* Frontend

2. **Anchor text is:**
   - *a.* Word or group of words, which is linked to a website/web page
   - *b.* Website or Web page to which the word is linked
   - *c.* The text that comes right before the word that is linked to a website/web page
   - *d.* None of these

3. **WordPress dashboard is the frontend:**
   - *a.* True
   - *b.* False

Answer Key

1. d   2. a   3. b

Take it Further

- o Check how the header of Google changes when you go to its search results page. What additional elements can you see in its header?

- o Notice how various websites, which you frequently use, look on different devices.

Chapter 5

Posts, Pages, and Your School Timetable

Structure Bot

In this chapter, we will discuss the following topics:

- ◆ Reviewing your school timetable
- ◆ What are posts?
- ◆ What are pages?
- ◆ Difference between posts and pages

*W*ordPress comes with a system or tools that enable you to build your website effectively. However, some of these tools may look very similar but could be very different. For example, Posts and Pages. Although they look the same when you start learning WordPress, they are completely different.

In this chapter, we will cover both of these topics and understand their use case with a little help from your school timetable.

Objective Bot

At the end of this chapter, you will:

- ◆ Have an intuitive understanding of both Posts and pages that are essential parts of building a website with WordPress
- ◆ Be able to decide whether a piece of content should be added as a post or page on your website

Reviewing your school timetable

The school timetable is important for every student. They act as a guide in your school life. Also, we are very excited when we see a PE/PT period in our timetable and a little sad when a Mathematics class comes up!

Your timetable may look something like the one shown in the following figure:

Timetable

Time	Monday	Tuesday	Wednesday	Thursday	Friday	Saturday
1						
2						
3						
4						
5						
6						
7						
8						

Figure 5.1: *A sample school timetable*

Your timetable may be a bit different or exactly like the one in *Figure 5.1*, depending on your school's format. Now, let's see how the classes are structured on a timetable. For example, you may have a school assembly at the start of the day, Mathematics as your first period, value education as your second period, and so on. Later, at some time during the middle of the day, you may have a lunch break.

Of the above things, there are two things on the timetable that keep repeating: School assembly and lunch break.

The sequence of other classes or the classes itself can change on different days, but these two will remain constant. For many schools, the first period may also be constant, which may be the class teacher's period. Do you get the idea? There are a few things on the timetable that don't change, while others keep changing.

This is on a weekly timetable. Even when you complete your year and move to a different class, these constant points on the timetable will still stay the same. It may happen only in 3-4 years or so that someone may change the timing of lunch break by 10 or 15 minutes. However, these changes are rare.

So, if we categorize, periods like school assembly and lunch break can be called **static** because they almost never change. Other periods can be called **dynamic** because they keep changing. Let us keep this example of static and dynamic in our minds as we move ahead in this chapter.

What are Posts?

Coming back to the topic, let us use the school timetable example to understand what posts are.

When you click on **Posts** in your sidebar menu, you will be taken to the page as shown in the following figure:

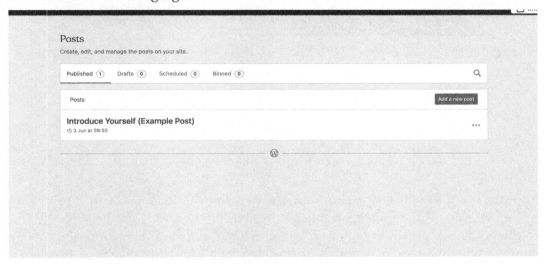

Figure 5.2: All Posts page on WordPress dashboard

The page shown in the preceding figure is the "*All Posts*" page on your WordPress dashboard. As you add posts, it will keep coming up here. You can see a default example Post in the figure as well. There is an option to "**Add a new post**" too, which we will explore in detail in the next chapter.

Now, let us understand posts. In our school timetable, most of the periods changed daily. We called them dynamic periods. Similarly, there will be a lot of content on your website that will keep coming regularly. They will be very dynamic in nature.

Let us take the example of *"The Times of India"* website:

Figure 5.3: The Times of India homepage

You can see different articles coming on *"The Times of India"*. The editorial team of the website or its reporters publish new articles every day on the website, and in many cases also edit the old articles that were published. This kind of dynamic content, which is regularly added or updated on a WordPress website, is called a post.

However, this example is not limited only to a website that deals with articles. If you have an e-commerce website, you will be adding new products or editing old products regularly. In that case, those products can also be categorized as posts. Any content that is added or edited on a regular basis are the posts on WordPress.

We have talked about E-commerce websites quite a few times. But what exactly is an e-commerce site? E-commerce stands for electronic commerce and represents the world of internet commerce – the new way to buy and sell things. Any website that sells any product or service online is an e-commerce website. The most popular example of an E-commerce website would be Amazon.

What are pages?

So, if Posts are dynamic content, what are Pages? Even on a dynamic website, such as *The Times of India*, there are many pages that are static in nature.

Let us take the example of its homepage. Even though you see new articles coming there daily, the nature of the homepage remains the same – it shows the latest articles on the page.

All the categories of articles shown on the homepage will remain static. Only the posts that are shown under those categories will change.

There can be individual pages for different categories too, as you can see on the menu of *The Times of India*. Clicking on those pages will take you to different pages, where it will show only the latest articles from that category.

There are many pages on a website where the content also does not change, such as the Terms of Use page, Privacy Policy page, and more. For example, you can see the "**Terms of Use**" page on The Times of India in the following figure:

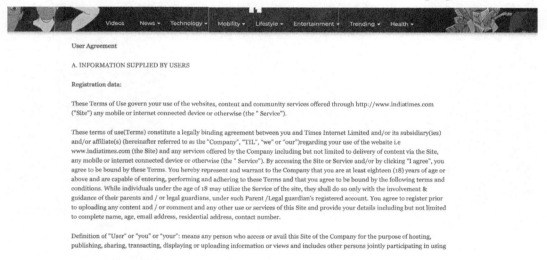

Figure 5.4: *Terms of Use page on The Times of India website*

Difference between Posts and Pages

We have already covered the key difference between Posts and Pages. Now, let us discuss it in more detail to make sure we perfectly understand it.

As we discussed before, Posts are meant for dynamic content, whereas Pages are meant for static content (the nature of the content on a page can be dynamic too).

This difference can easily be seen on *"The Times of India"* website if we open their **Terms of Use** page and one article on the website. It is quite evident that the new **Terms of Use** page is not being added every day, whereas the new articles are being added on a daily basis.

However, the difference between Posts and Pages blurs a bit when we call the homepage of "The Times of India" as a Page and an article on it as a Post. The homepage also changes on a daily basis as new articles come on the website. Also, we earlier said that the nature of the homepage remains the same – It shows the static content.

Let us explore this concept with one more example. Imagine you walk into a bookstore like the one in *Figure 5.5*:

Figure 5.5: Representation of a bookstore

You go into the bookshop and see different books. If you get out of the bookshop and come again after a few days, you will notice some changes. That is because the books you may have seen on your earlier visit would have been replaced with new books.

The books come and go from the bookshop. That causes a bit of change in the look and feel of the bookshop but that does not necessarily change the bookshop itself. The bookshop still remains at the same address, it will have the identical surface area, wall color, and still displays the popular books. The nature of the bookstore remains the same. Will it be wrong to say that the bookstore remains static, whereas books that come and go to/from the bookstore are dynamic?

The different articles on *"The Times of India"* are just like books. And the homepage acts as a bookstore. And if we say bookstores are static, then by the same logic, *"The Times of India"* homepage is also static even though its content might change from time to time.

Recap

Posts and Pages are the tools you will use for creating content on your website for your visitors. In this chapter, we understood the key differences between the two, and we also learned when to use one over the other for different use cases.

It is important to intuitively grasp the difference between them so that when you are creating your website, you know exactly what you have to create – A Post or a Page.

Points to Remember

- Any content that is added or edited on a regular basis is generally called a post on WordPress.

- Pages are used for the content, which is static in nature.

- A Page can also show new content on a regular basis, but the nature of the Page remains static.

- Pages are just like bookstores. Even though books come and go to/from a bookstore, which changes it a bit, the nature of the bookstore remains static, that is it remains at the same place as ever. It is the books that keep changing.

Multiple Choice Questions

1. **Page is used for dynamic content:**

    a. True

    a. False

2. **Which one of these is most likely to be a Post?**

    a. A news update

    b. Contact Us Page

    c. Homepage

    d. Privacy Policy

3. **Is the content on a Page always static?**

    a. Yes

    b. No

Answer Key

| 1. | b | | 2. | a | | 3. | b |

Take it Further

o Think of a few more websites and categorize their content as posts or pages.

Chapter 6

Creating Your First Post

Structure Bot

In this chapter, we will discuss the following topics:

- Adding a post
- Exploring different blocks
- Inserting images
- Publishing a post
- Editing a post
- Formatting a post

*W*e understood the difference between posts and pages in the last chapter quite clearly. In this chapter, we will learn to create posts on our very own website. Being able to create a post will provide us the power to add as much content as required on our website on a regular basis.

This will keep our website visitors engaged with useful content. And therefore, they will keep coming back to our website for new content and also tell their friends about it. This will lead to an increase in our web traffic over time. If you have already learned how to read bar charts as asked in the *"Take it Further"* section of *Chapter 3, Setting Up Your Site* , then this is how your traffic bar chart may look like

during a one year period. With the consistent posting of new content your users like, your traffic should steadily keep increasing, as shown in the following figure:

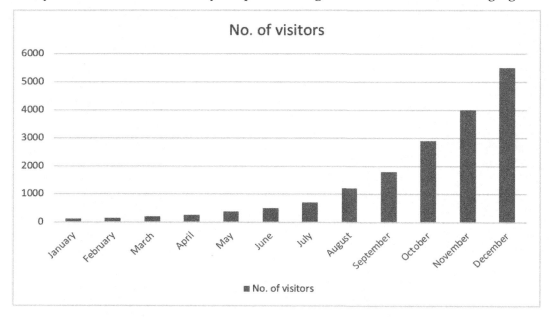

Figure 6.1: *Website traffic chart*

Let us see how we can create a post and make this a reality.

At the end of this chapter, you will:

◆ Be equipped with the power of creating Posts on your website

◆ Be able to create, edit, and enrich your Posts with a number of features available on your WordPress dashboard

Adding a post

To create a post, click on **Posts** on your sidebar menu. If you click on **Posts** directly, you will be taken to the "**All Posts**" page, which looks like the following image:

Figure 6.2: *All Posts Page*

You can then click on the "**Add a new post**" button to access the **Add Post** page. You can also hover on **Posts** in the sidebar menu and directly click on "**Add New**" to reach the **Add Post** page. This will help you navigate directly to the **Add Post** page in the future without coming to the **All Posts** page, which may save some time. The **Add Post** page will look something like this (refer to *Figure 6.3*):

Figure 6.3: *Add Post Page*

The most evident option here is to add a title. After "**Add title**", it is mentioned, "**Start writing or type/to choose a block**".

Exploring blocks

A block is a piece of content, which may contain a paragraph, image, video, or any other type of content. You can add new blocks or select the type of content that goes into a block.

To begin with, let us add a title to our post. To enter the title, simply click on the area where "**Add title**" is mentioned and start writing. Once you have entered the title, this is how it will look (refer to *Figure 6.4*):

Figure 6.4: *Add Post page after adding title*

Let us try adding a couple of blocks to our post. Click on "**Start writing or type / to choose a block**" and start writing. You can enter 2-3 sentences about how your experience has been so far using WordPress.

After you are done writing your content in the first block, press *Enter* and WordPress will automatically create a new block for you. Start writing again in the second block. You can mention about the different features you have explored so far on WordPress in this block. When you are done writing, your editor will have content in the following format:

Figure 6.5: *Add Post page after adding text*

Previewing the post

You can see "**Preview**" highlighted in a red box in *Figure 6.5*. This option allows you to see how your post will look like when it is live on the website without actually making it live. Let us click on that button and have a look at it:

Figure 6.6: Previewing a Post

You can see in this box how your post will look to your website visitors. You can even select your device to see how it would be rendered differently on desktop, mobile, and tablets. You have a drop down on the top left to select this option.

When you are done previewing the post, you can close the preview and go back to the editor by clicking on "**Close**" on the top left.

Now, let us try adding an image to our Post.

Adding an image block

To add a new image, we need to create a new block. As we have seen before, we can create a new block simply by pressing enter when we have finished working on a block. But let us try doing it in a different way this time.

Notice the + symbol on the top left in *Figure 6.5*. Click on it. When you click on the + icon, a sidebar menu kind of window will come up, which will have a lot of different options as follows:

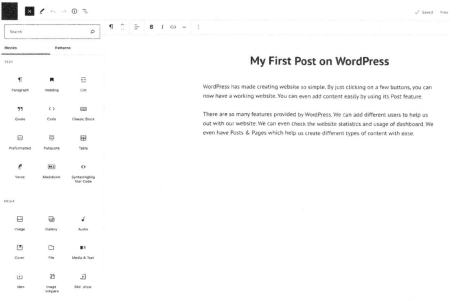

Figure 6.7: *Different blocks you can add in a post*

We will select the **Image** from the **Media** section. While hovering over other options, note how WordPress gives you a prompt of what that option can do.

After clicking the image option, a new block will automatically appear, which will show an option for adding an image to your post as shown in *Figure 6.8*:

Figure 6.8: *Add image option in the Image block*

After you have this option, you can even close your side window by clicking on the X icon at the same place where there was a + icon earlier. There are various ways you can add an image to your post. You can select an image from your WordPress account media library, you can add a URL of any image from the internet, or you can upload an image from your laptop.

We will go with the last option, although you can try the other two as well. But we don't have any images in our WordPress media library yet as we haven't added any images through our WordPress account. Once you start adding images from your WordPress account, you can later select them directly from your media library. You can, however, also try adding an Image URL.

To upload an image, click on the **Upload** button and select an image file from your laptop that you want to upload. We have added the WordPress homepage image, but you can add any depending on the kind of post you are writing.

After you select an image from your laptop, the image will be added to your post, and you will have an option to enter a caption for the image. You can add the caption as per the image and the post you are writing. After we are done, our post would look like the following figure, and yours would look similar, although obviously with your text and image:

Figure 6.9: Post after adding an image

Wrapping up and publishing our post

Before we publish our post, let us add one more paragraph to it. You now know how to add a new block. Click on + icon on the top left and select paragraph to add a new paragraph block if it isn't already there in your post. Once you do that, let us begin writing another 2-3 sentences in this new paragraph block.

Once you are done typing, we will publish the post. To publish the post, click on the "**Publish**" button on the top right, as shown in the previous figure.

When you click on **Publish**, WordPress will ask for a confirmation of whether you are sure about publishing the post. Then, click on **Publish** again and your post will be published, and WordPress will show you the link of your post as shown in the following figure:

Figure 6.10: *Fetching post link*

The title of your post shown on the top right in *Figure 6.10* is now present instead of a **Publish** button. This title is hyperlinked to your post on the website. You can click on it to open your post, or copy paste the link of your post in your browser from the Post address box.

Figure 6.11 shows how the post we published looks on the website:

Figure 6.11: *Published post on a website*

So, there you go! You have published your first post on WordPress. That is quite an achievement. You are now fully equipped to provide valuable content to your website visitors.

Editing a post

After publishing the post, close the right sidebar that had publishing details by clicking on the X button on the top right side. When you do so, you can notice that the **Publish** button has now become the **Update** button as follows:

Figure 6.12: *Update button while editing a Post*

This is because you are not adding a post, but you are editing a post now. A post that has been published can be altered by editing it and clicking on the **Update** button. You have all the same functions available with you while editing as you had while publishing the post.

Alternatively, if you close the tab, then you can reach this edit page by clicking on **Posts** on your sidebar, then clicking on three vertical dots on the right side of this Post and selecting the **Edit** option as shown in the following figure:

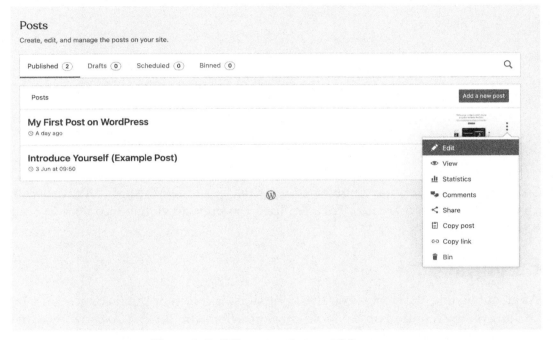

Figure 6.13: Edit post option on All Posts page

We will try out a few more options while we edit our post. However, note that these same options will also be available when you publish a new post.

Trying out new blocks

Let us try out the quote block. Select the "**Quote**" block by clicking on the + sign on the top left. Enter any quotation you like, who said it or where you read it in the citation part. It will be displayed as shown in the following figure:

WordPress Homepage

WordPress has enabled many of the leading websites to create highly scalable products for their users. It is no joke that more than 40-50% of the websites in the world are powered by WordPress. That is a testament to the power of this platform.

> ## Code is Poetry.
>
> - WordPress tagline

WordPress has been using Code is Poetry tagline since a long time. And rightly so! Code is indeed the poetry of the new world driven by technology.

Figure 6.14: Checking out the Quote block

I have entered "**Code is Poetry**" as the quote, which Matt, one of the creators of WordPress, has been saying for a long time. And I believe it is right. Code is indeed the poetry of the new world driven by technology.

There are a number of other types of blocks available. You can yourself try some of them and see what they do. However, the basic idea is the same. You select a type of block, add the required parameters, and it automatically sets it up.

We will now click on the **Update** button on the top right side and the post will be updated on our website.

Formatting the post

Till now, we have covered various ways of adding a new type of content. But what if we want to change the properties of the existing content, such as its color, size, and more?

We will now cover how we can format our post.

To change the formatting, select a block. In the following image, we have selected the first block. To select a block, you have to click on it, as shown in *Figure 6.15*:

Figure 6.15: Formatting options

In the right sidebar, notice how the options have changed. It displays the properties of this block, which can be modified. For example, try changing the font size of the text in this block. Click on the `Font size` dropdown and select `Medium`. You can also set custom font size by specifying its pixel size in the custom box.

To change the color, click on any color or get more color options by clicking on `Custom` color. You also have the option to change the background color of text or link colors in that block.

There is also one option at the bottom called **Drop Cap**. If you select that option, the first letter of your block will be made relatively larger compared with other text.

The following figure shows how our post looks like after we made some of the changes as discussed:

My First Post on WordPress

WordPress has made creating website so simple. By just clicking on a few buttons, you can now have a working website. You can even add content easily by using its Post feature.

There are so many features provided by WordPress. We can add different users to help us out with our website. We can even check the website statistics and usage of dashboard. We even have Posts & Pages which help us create different types of content with ease.

Welcome to the world's most popular website builder.

Figure 6.16: Post after formatting the text

The following figure shows how the options change when we select the image block:

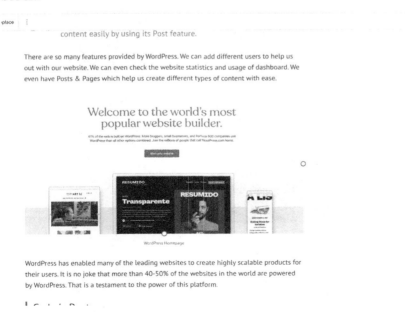

Figure 6.17: Formatting options for Image block

You can see how the options on the right side change when we select an image block. Like the text block, you can set the size of the image here by changing its width and height from the Image dimension section. Or you can use a preset size by directly selecting a size from the **Image size** dropdown.

You can also style your image and make them have rounded edges by selecting **Rounded** from the styles section. Feel free to experiment with different options.

However, there is one field called "**Alt text**" there, which wouldn't really modify the look and feel of the image on the website. So, what is it used for?

It is recommended to add **Alt text** in all the images on your website unless the image is just for decorative purposes and has no context on the page. For example, Alt text is used for visually impaired people. They may use voice readers to check out web pages, and Alt text provides them with the required description of the image.

But **Alt text** has even more use cases nowadays. For example, your Internet maybe slow and is unable to load images, or you may have disabled the loading of images. In that case, instead of the image, you will see the **Alt text**, which will still explain to you the context of the image.

When you are done adding these fields, you can click on the **Update** button on the top right side. The following figure shows how our final post looks like on our website:

Figure 6.18: Final post after publishing

In this chapter, we have covered the basics of how to create a post on WordPress. First, we went through the concept of blocks and added a few blocks ourselves. Then, while editing the post, we even experimented with different formatting options.

But this doesn't end here. Now that you are aware of the concept of blocks and have created a few yourselves, it is time for you to experiment with a number of other blocks available on WordPress. For example, try to add a Video block or a Table block and see how options change. There is a lot to explore, and your journey has just begun.

Points to Remember

- You can click on the "**Add a new post**" button on the **All Posts** page to access the **Add Post** page. You can also hover on **Posts** in the sidebar menu and directly click on "**Add New**" to reach the **Add Post** page.

- A block is a piece of content, which may contain a paragraph, image, video, or any other type of content.

- There are various ways you can add an image to your post. For example, you can select an image from your WordPress account media library, you can add a URL of any image from the internet, or you can upload an image from your laptop.

- To access formatting options, select a block by clicking on it and formatting options will come on the right.

- The Drop Cap option makes the first letter relatively larger compared with other text in the block.

- Alt text is used for visually impaired people. They may use voice readers to check out web pages, and Alt text provides them with the required description of the image.

Multiple Choice Questions

1. Which one of these is not a type of block?
   - *a.* A paragraph
   - *b.* Image
   - *c.* Post title
   - *d.* Post subheading

2. Is it possible to preview a post before publishing it?
   - *a.* Yes
   - *b.* No

3. You can add only 4 blocks in a post:
   - *a.* Yes
   - *b.* No

4. Option to format different blocks of post is not available while publishing a post:
   - *a.* Yes
   - *b.* No

5. Alt Text is not used for:
   - *a.* Visually impaired people
   - *b.* For showing image description in case the image is not loaded
   - *c.* Making the image look nicer
   - *d.* None of these

Answer Key

1. c   2. a   3. b   4. b   5. c

Take it Further

o Explore other types of blocks on WordPress while creating a post and notice how the formatting options change for different blocks

Chapter 7

Comments, Categories, and Tags

Structure Bot

In this chapter, we will discuss the following topics:

- ◆ Comments
- ◆ Categories
- ◆ Tags

*I*n the earlier chapters, we covered what posts are, their usage, and how to create them. But does it make sense to write a post on your website without categorizing it or not allowing people to discuss around your post?

As the number of posts grows on your website and your traffic increases, you will want these features. And the good news is that WordPress has already got these covered for you.

Objective Bot

At the end of this chapter, you will:

- ◆ Build upon your ability to create a post, and equip yourself with more features that can be used to enrich the posts on your website

- ◆ Enable/disable comments and categorize/tag posts on your websites

Comments

When you are sitting around with your friends and having a chat, how would it be if you were the only one speaking? Will it feel lively not to hear back the opinion of your friends? Absolutely not! Conversations or discussions are interesting because everyone gets to speak their mind.

No matter whether your friend's opinion is aligned with yours or not, you would still want to hear it. Even when your father or mother read the news, they tend to discuss it among themselves or with their friends because that is what we humans do! We discuss things with each other and that is why we have been able to grow as a community over the last hundreds of thousands of years.

When you write a post on your website, in most cases, you would want the same. You will want to see how the world perceives your post. And the best way to do so is by allowing them to comment on it. They can post their feedback or opinion or anything they want to add through comments.

Even when you post a picture or update it on *Facebook* or *Instagram*, your friends can comment on it. So, why not do the same on your website too?

If you would have noticed, the comments were already active in the post that we published in the last chapter. So, at the bottom of the post on the website, you will find the comment section:

Figure 7.1: Comment box in our post

As you are signed in to your *WordPress.com* account, you are commenting using that profile. This is just how you comment on *Facebook* and *Instagram* using your profile. Further in this chapter, we will see how we can configure these options on our WordPress dashboard.

A commenter can also select to get notifications of new comments or notifications about new posts on this website via email. All they have to do is tick the corresponding field against that and then click on **Post Comment** while commenting.

Adding a comment

Let us add a comment from our profile on the post and see how it comes up. To add the comment, write something in the comment box and then click on **Post Comment**. Here is how it looks:

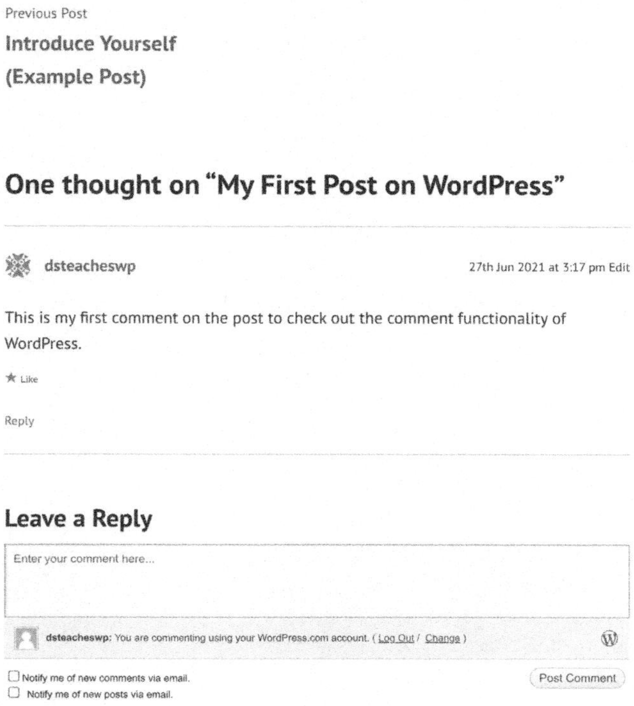

Previous Post
Introduce Yourself
(Example Post)

One thought on "My First Post on WordPress"

dsteacheswp   27th Jun 2021 at 3:17 pm Edit

This is my first comment on the post to check out the comment functionality of WordPress.

★ Like

Reply

Leave a Reply

Enter your comment here...

dsteacheswp: You are commenting using your WordPress.com account. (Log Out / Change)

☐ Notify me of new comments via email.
☐ Notify me of new posts via email.

Post Comment

Figure 7.2: Comment on a post

Notice how the comment has come up under the heading – One thought on **"My First Post on WordPress"**. Other website visitors can even directly reply to this comment. They can do so if they want to take part in this comment discussion instead of adding a new comment.

But how did the comment section come on our post by default? Will this happen always or do we have control over whether we want to show a comment section on a post or not? We absolutely do!

Enabling or disabling comments

Whether you want someone to comment on one of your posts or not is totally your decision. But after having discussed so many benefits of comments, you may be wondering why you would want to disable it. Well, sometimes, you may want to do so depending upon the post you are writing. For example, if you are writing on a sensitive topic that may attract outrage from certain people, you may want to disable comments so that they do not spread any hatred.

This is why few social media sites, such as *Facebook*, have also now provided this feature of disabling comments on a post. Most of the time, you may want to have a discussion, but a discussion is only helpful when it is done with the right spirit.

So, how do we enable or disable a comment? First, let us go back to the `Edit Post` page of the post we published in the last chapter:

Figure 7.3: Settings icon on Edit Post page

Do you note the wheel icon in the red box? That is your settings icon. Click on it, and you will be able to see these options:

Figure 7.4: *Allow comments option in settings sidebar*

Click on **Discussion** from the different options on the right, and you will be able to see **Allow comments** field as shown in the preceding figure. By default, **Allow comments** is auto-selected. If you want to disable comments on your post, you have to unselect it and then click on the **Update** button to the right side on the top.

The following figure shows how the comment section of our post looks on the website when we unselect the **Allow comments** and update our post:

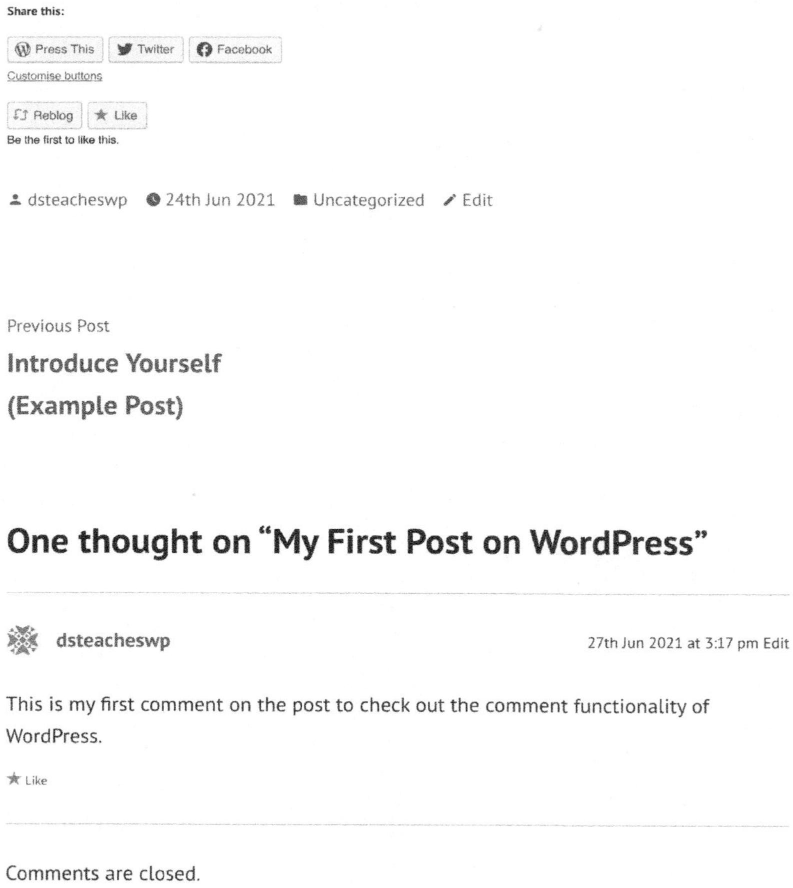

Share this:

W Press This   🐦 Twitter   f Facebook

Customise buttons

↻ Reblog   ★ Like

Be the first to like this.

👤 dsteacheswp   🕐 24th Jun 2021   📁 Uncategorized   ✎ Edit

Previous Post

Introduce Yourself

(Example Post)

One thought on "My First Post on WordPress"

▓ **dsteacheswp**   27th Jun 2021 at 3:17 pm Edit

This is my first comment on the post to check out the comment functionality of WordPress.

★ Like

Comments are closed.

Figure 7.5: Closed comments on the post

In the preceding figure, you can see that the comment we had posted before is present, but the option to add new comments is not visible anymore. It is also mentioned that "**Comments are closed.**".

This is how we enable or disable comments on the post. And we have also seen that how our visitors can add a comment on a post.

But how do we decide who can add a comment? Depending upon the type of the website we are building, we may only want people to add a comment if they provide their basic details, or we may want everyone to comment. WordPress allows you to configure these settings at once throughout your website.

Comment settings

To access comment settings, hover over "**Settings**" on the left sidebar menu on the dashboard and click on "**Discussion**", and you can see the following screenshot:

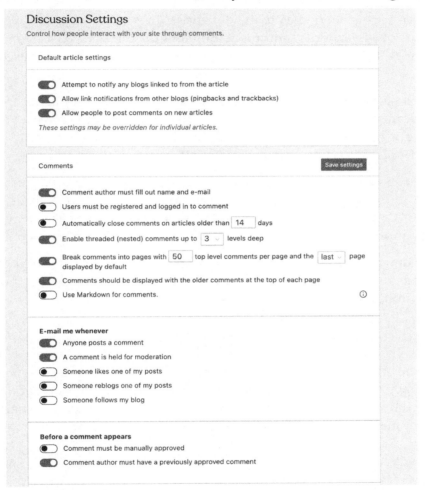

Figure 7.6: Configuring comment settings on your website

You can see a lot of setting options. All the options are controlled by a toggle switch. If the toggle switch is blue, the answer to settings is yes, otherwise its no. For example, consider the third settings in the Default article settings section – "**Allow people to post comments on new articles**". You can see the switch is blue here, so by default, people can comment on any new post we add. If you click on the toggle switch, then this setting will change, and people won't be able to comment on any new post by default.

You remember how the comment section appeared by default on our post. That was because of this setting. For the three settings in the `Default article settings` section, these can be overridden for individual articles, and that is why we were able to disable comments on our post.

These three settings here dictate the default settings when a new post is created, but they can be overridden and made different for different posts. Among these three settings, there is only one setting for comments, so we have focused only on that.

In the next section, you can find more options related to comments specifically. Here you can select options that decide whether a user should have a WordPress. com account before they can comment. Or should they compulsorily add their name and email ids before they can comment or not.

You can also set a comment approval process. For example, if you want the comment to be approved before it appears publicly on your website, you can enable the "`Comment must be manually approved`" setting. This way, you will be able to approve every comment on your website before it appears publicly.

You can configure all the above settings as per your liking. The settings will be auto-saved, but you can click on the "`Save settings`" button in case you do not receive a prompt about settings being saved.

Approving/rejecting a comment

If you do not allow comments to be automatically approved, then you will have to manually approve comments before they are displayed publicly on your post. To check out the recently posted comments on your website, click on **Comments** in the left sidebar menu on the dashboard, as shown in the following figure:

Figure 7.7: Comment approval page

Whenever a new comment is added to your website, you will be able to check them here. For example, to check only the pending comments (comments that are pending for your approval), you can click on **Pending** (next to All tab where we are present right now) and you will be able to see those comments.

To approve a comment, you will have to click on the **Approve** button. If you want to delete a comment, we can click on the "**Bin**" button and the comment will be deleted.

We have now learned the different ways to manage comments on our website. This will enable you to moderate discussions effectively, which will ultimately increase the quality of content on your website.

Categories

To understand categories, let us go back and discuss the bookstore example further that we encountered in *Chapter 5, Posts, Pages, and Your School Timetable*. When you walk into a bookstore, the books are often categorized according to the genres. Suppose you want to purchase a Science book, you can directly go to the science section and checkout the collection there.

A bookstore has a few categorical sections like that. Depending on the size of the bookstore, the number of categories might be more or less. However, whichever new book comes into the bookstore is assigned to a category from the categories present at the bookstore. The store may have a *"General"* or *"Other"* category for books that may not be a part of any specific category that they have.

Similarly, on your website, you too would want to categorize your content. This will make it easier for your visitors to find the type of content they are interested in.

As we will have a limited number of posts on the website when we launch, we can create limited categories only. We can increase the number of categories as the number of posts on the website increases.

As we are building a website around this book and the topic *"WordPress"*, we may add the following categories to our website:

- **Tutorials**: This is to share tutorials about how to do something on WordPress

- **News**: This is to share the latest news/announcements about WordPress

- **General**: This is to share general information/articles about WordPress

You can also create a list of categories depending upon the kind of website you are building.

Adding a category

To add a category, hover over **Posts** in your sidebar menu on the dashboard and click on **Categories**. You should see a page with the list of categories on your website:

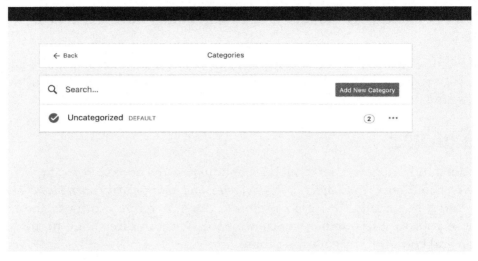

Figure 7.8: Categories on your website

To add a new category, click on the "**Add New Category**" button. Next, you will see a box for adding category details:

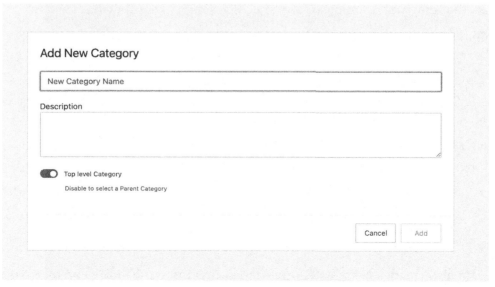

Figure 7.9: Add Category box

Enter the name of your category, add its description, and then click on **Add**. Do this for all the categories that you want.

After you have added all the categories, you will be able to see them all on this page:

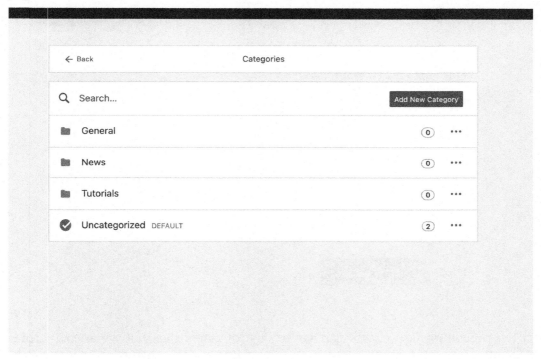

Figure 7.10: Active categories on your website

Okay, so we have now added **Categories** to our website, but how do we connect our Posts with these categories?

Once you have connected the Post with categories, you will be able to see the number of Posts in a category in the oval box against each category. They currently show "0" and Uncategorized category shows as "2". This is so because both the posts on our website have been connected with Uncategorized category as it was the default one.

Now that we have created our own category let us connect the post published in the last chapter with these categories.

Adding categories to a post

Open the edit page of the post that we created in the last chapter and click on the settings icon as we did earlier in this chapter. Then, open the categories section from the settings sidebar, as seen in the figure:

Figure 7.11: Selecting categories while adding/editing a post

In the preceding figure, you can see the list of categories that we added earlier. We will select "**General**" for this post as it does not qualify to be a part of the other two categories. We will also unselect **Uncategorized** now. You can select the category accordingly for your post.

You can see the "**Add New Category**" option here too. You can use it to create a new category while adding/editing a new post if you don't have a particular category. However, because you won't often create categories, you can do it how we did it in this chapter earlier because it is more convenient to do it that way.

Once you have selected the relevant categories for this post, you can click on the **Update** button. In the coming chapters, we will see how we can use these categories to make it easier for our visitors to find the post they might be interested in.

In the settings of post, you can find an option: Featured Image. Featured Image is a representative image for your Post. While you can add multiple images in your post, you can select/upload only one image as Featured Image. This will be used to represent your post when it is shared on social media or when it is listed (like on homepage/categories page) on your website. Go ahead and add a Featured Image to your post using this option and then update the post.

Tags

Let us again come back to our bookstore example. Earlier, we saw how categorizing books by genre makes it easier for us to find books in a bookstore. For example, if you want to find a Science book, you can directly go to the science section. The physical world has its limitation, though. It can allow such categorization only to a certain extent.

What if you want to find books that talk about comets? That is a very specific topic. In the physical world, you will have to surf through all the books in the science section and find a book on the comet. Or if the library is big enough, it may have a section around Astronomy, and you may find this book there.

However, this becomes a lot easier in the digital world through Tags. And the good news is most of the bookstores too are becoming digitized these days. So, if a new book comes into the bookstore and it is about comets, which may not be an exact category, here is what can be done. The bookstore can name the category as Science and add the following tags for the book in its digital system – Comets, Space, Extraterrestrial object, and so on.

Now, when you use the digital system of the bookstore, you can enter "**Comets**". And the bookstore will provide you the list of available books around "*Comets*" with their exact location.

While categories are defined and limited in number, tags can be unlimited. Categories are used to broadly categorize something in certain buckets. Tags are used for more specific categorization. Imagine tags to be like keywords about a product. For books, it can be any topic that the book is about or the name of the author, anything that a person may use to search that book.

In WordPress, you can use tags to add specific keywords about a post that a person may use to reach that post.

Adding tags to a post

Let us go back to the Edit page of our post, open settings, and select **Tags**, as shown here:

Figure 7.12: Adding Tags while adding/editing a post

We can directly add Tags to a post here. To add multiple tags, you can keep entering them separated by commas or press enter after adding each tag.

Here are the tags to be added to this post: WordPress, WordPress features, Posts & Pages. You can add multiple tags in your post with whichever keywords you find relevant for your Post.

Once you add a tag in one of your Posts, for example, WordPress, all the Posts that will have this tag in the future can be grouped together. So, when a person reaches this tag page on our website, he/she will be able to find all Posts with this tag in one place. We will find how to do this in upcoming chapters.

The following figure shows how it will look after adding the tags:

Figure 7.13: *Tags added on the add/edit post page*

Once you have added your tags, click on **Update**, and these tags will be added to your Post. You can also see a list of tags on your website and the number of Posts against those tags. Hover over Posts in the sidebar on your dashboard, and click on **Tags**. You can find this list as shown in *Figure 7.14*:

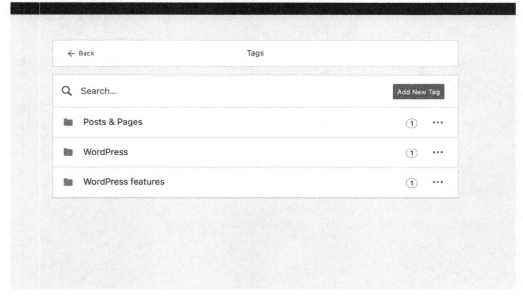

Figure 7.14: *All tags on our website*

Recap

In this chapter, we covered how we can enable discussion on our website to engage users. This engagement will ultimately help increase the overall quality of content on the website in the long term. We also learned how to categorize content to make it easier for our users to find it. While categories help us to classify the content in limited categories broadly, tags help us to do that more specifically.

In the next chapter, we will start exploring pages and see how we can create one.

Points to Remember

- Comments allow users to add their feedback or opinion to your post. They can also add anything to the information you have already provided in the post through comments.

- You can enable or disable comments for individual posts.

- You can set up a comment approval process for any comment posted on your website. If approval is required, a comment will be made public only when you have approved it from your dashboard.

- Categories allow you to broadly classify content on your website, making it easier for users to find them.

- Tags are like keywords. They are unlimited and help you classify content more specifically.

Multiple Choice Questions

1. Only signed-in users can comment on WordPress sites:
   a. True
   b. False
   c. Can be true or false – Depends on our settings
   d. None of these

2. A comment is useful for:
   a. Getting feedback from users
   b. Hearing the opinion of users on your post
   c. Allowing users to add missing/extra information to your post
   d. All of these

3. You can't add categories as tags:
   a. True
   b. False

4. You can only have 4 categories on your website:
   a. True
   b. False

Answer Key

1. c   2. d   3. b   4. b

Take it Further

o Google and read more about tags and keywords. Read how they make searching content easier for users.

Chapter 8

Creating a Page

Structure Bot

In this chapter, we will discuss the following topics:

- ◆ Creating a page
- ◆ Using pre-defined layouts
- ◆ Editing a layout
- ◆ Adding new blocks
- ◆ Exploring various block options

In *Chapter 5, Posts, Pages and Your School Timetable*, we learned the difference between posts and pages. But until now, we only discussed how to create and segregate posts using categories and tags. It is time to move ahead from posts and learn how to create a page.

Websites are not only about dynamic content that we add from time to time. There are many pages on a website, which stay static, such as its Homepage or About Me/Us page. In this chapter, we will learn how to create these kinds of static pages.

Objective Bot

At the end of this chapter, you will:

- ◆ Learn to create static pages on your website
- ◆ Be comfortable using different layout options on WordPress to build beautiful pages

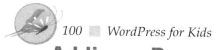

Adding a Page

To add a new page, hover over **Pages** on your left sidebar menu and click on the "**Add New**" button. As you click on **Add New**, you will be taken to a page where you will be shown various options to select a layout, as shown in the following figure:

Figure 8.1: Various layout options

There are a lot of pre-defined layouts available. You can design your page from scratch by clicking on the **Blank Page** button, but selecting a pre-defined layout makes designing easier. WordPress has a huge collection of pre-defined layouts, which you can surf through by selecting categories on the left.

We will create an "**About Me**" page for the website. So the first option on this page itself seems to match our requirements. You can select the one that is most suitable for you.

After selecting the layout, the demo content from the layout is loaded into the editor, as shown in the following figure:

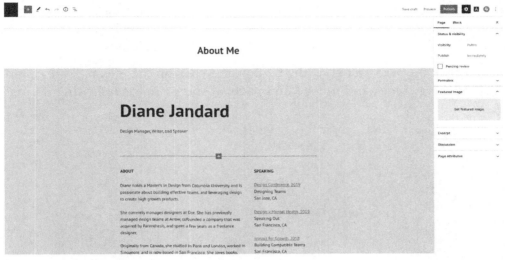

Figure 8.2: *Content loaded from the layout in Page editor*

The editor for pages is almost identical to the editor for posts. And you will find that the same options are available for pages too.

The building components for a page are blocks, just like posts. If you want to add a new piece of content to this existing layout, you can add a new block by clicking on the + button. First, let us edit the content in this layout according to our requirements. To edit the content, simply click on the **Block** and remove/add/ edit the content. Here is how the page looks after editing:

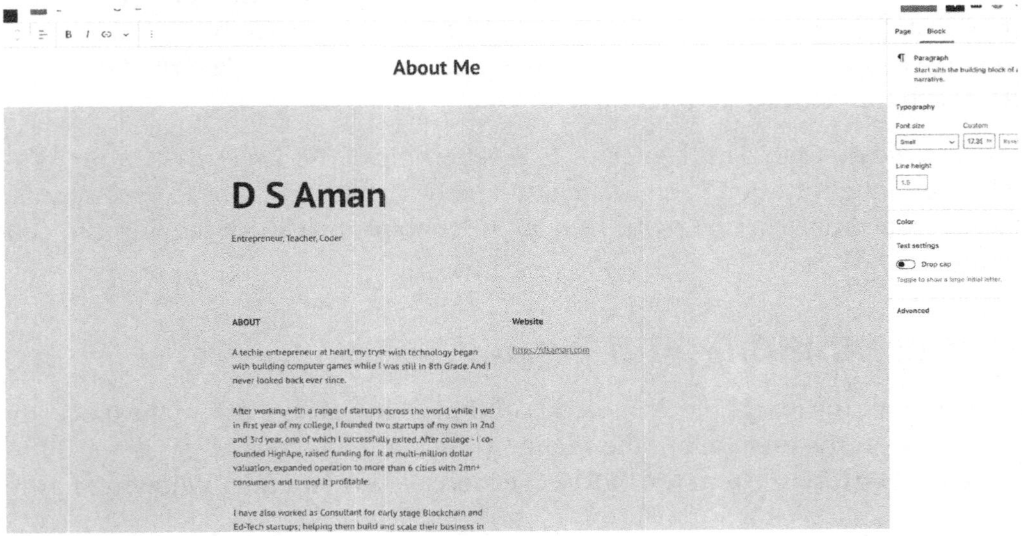

Figure 8.3: *Page after we have edited the demo text from the layout*

You can also change the formatting of any block. Click on the block and customize it from the right sidebar, as we did for posts. Let us add a new block to this existing layout. We will add an image below the name and the tagline.

You can click on the area below the tagline and click on the + icon to add a block. Select the image block and upload an image, as shown in the following figure:

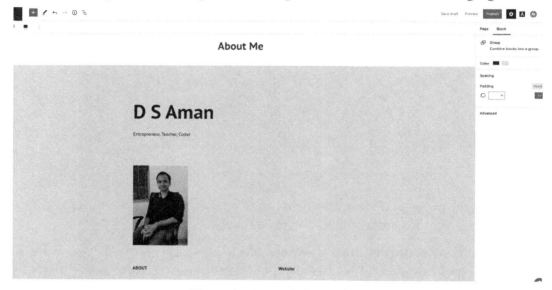

Figure 8.4: Image in Page editor

We have added an image, but the image looks out of place because of empty spaces on the right. It would look better if we add more images to the right, just as we have two columns of content below the image. One with the "**About**" title and the other with the "**Website**" title.

How can we do that? This brings us to a new topic of discussion – "Columns". In web designing, we often have to break our content into columns to accommodate spacing concerns. This helps us add more content instead of leaving the space empty.

Adding columns in a page

Let us remove the image block and add columns. First, delete the image block, then again click on the area below the tagline to select it. Next, click on the + button, and select "**Columns**" from the **DESIGN** section, as shown in the following figure:

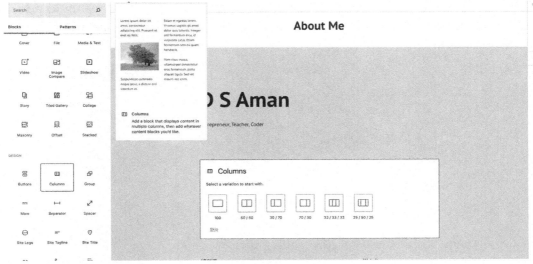

Figure 8.5: Selecting column options after choosing column design block

When you do that, you can see a new block with many options. They allow you to split the screen into different proportions. The following are the available options:

- **100:** This is the default selection. By default, a block takes up 100% of the space in width.

- **50/50:** This will allow you to split your screen into two columns in 50:50 proportion. This means that both the columns will take 50% space, one on the left and the other on the right.

- **30/70:** This will split the screen into two columns in 30:70 proportion. The first column will take 30% of the width and the other will take 70%.

- **70/30:** Same as 30/70 but vice versa. The first column will take 70% width and the other will take 30%.

- **33/33/33:** This will allow you to split your screen into 3 columns of equal proportions. Each column will take 33% of the screen.

- **25/50/25:** This will split your screen into 3 columns of unequal proportion. The first and third columns will take 25% width, whereas the second column will take 50% width.

We will go ahead with 33/33/33 for our use case. This will allow us to add 3 images next to each other. The following figure shows how 3 columns come up after we select 33/33/33:

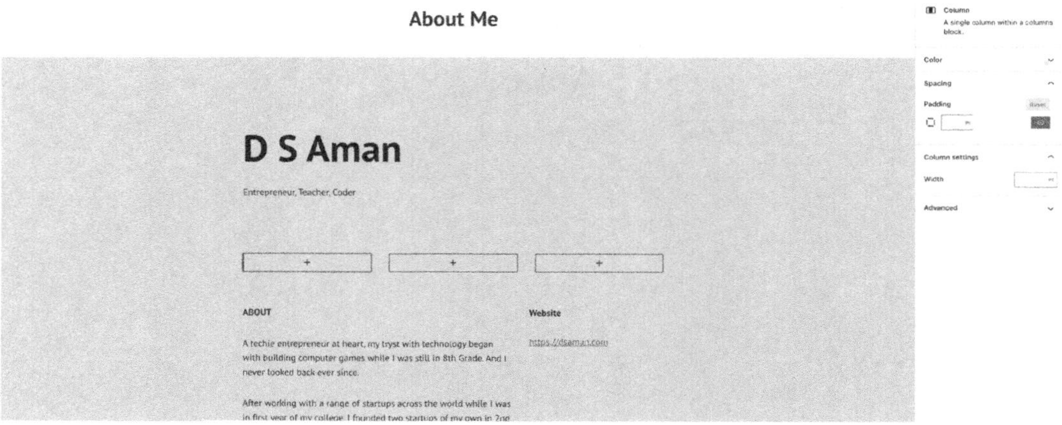

Figure 8.6: Three columns in the editor

We can now add different blocks to each column by clicking on it. Click on these columns, select the image block for each, and upload the images. You can alter the height and width of the image after uploading by selecting the image and altering its width or height from the right sidebar. This is how it looks after adding the images:

Figure 8.7: Page in the editor after adding images

Columns are very important when designing pages. We can also add these columns in posts in a similar way, although they are mostly used for pages.

WordPress automatically keeps saving your Post/Page when you are working on it. Even if you have not published a Post/Page, and accidentally closed the tab, you can go to All Posts/All Pages page and find the saved Post/Page in Drafts tab.

Let us publish this page now. The following is a small preview of our page on the website:

Figure 8.8: Preview of Page on Website

All the other options for pages remain the same as for posts. You can experiment and use more blocks here that you may not have explored previously. Try using as many blocks as possible as it will expand your thoughts and provide you more creative liberty to try out new things.

Recap

Creating a Page is not very different from creating a Post. We have the same options available. But while creating a Page, we need to put in more effort for designing it. This is so because a Page is static and will be viewed much more than a Post, which keeps coming on the website regularly and maybe outdated after a few days.

In this chapter, we covered a new block that helps us design content on our Page. The same can also be used for Posts. Feel free to explore more blocks from the design section, and in general too.

Now that we have understood how to create both static and dynamic content, we will now shift our focus to designing the website. We saw how columns help us modify the design of a Page or Post. In the next chapter, we will cover themes that will help us revamp the design of our whole website.

Points to Remember

- The editor for pages is almost exactly the same as the for posts. You can use the same blocks.

- There are a lot of pre-defined layouts available while building a page. You can design your page from scratch by clicking on the Blank Page button, but a pre-defined layout makes the job easier.

- Columns help you add more content blocks in the same row.

- You can divide a row of content into different blocks of different proportions.

- The following options are available while adding columns: 100, 50/50, 30/70, 70/30, 33/33/33, 25/50/25.

Multiple Choice Questions

1. **You cannot add images next to each other:**

    a. True

    b. False

2. **What is the difference between a Paragraph block and a Column block?**

    a. One is a text type block, while the other is a design type block

    b. Both do the same thing

    c. Column block is used for adding images, while the paragraph is used for adding text

    d. None of these

3. **Any kind of media/text block can be added in different columns:**

    a. True

    b. False

4. **25/50/25 column type will divide the row into how many columns:**

    a. 1

    b. 3

    c. 25

    d. 2

Answer Key

1. b   2. a   3. a   4. b

Take it Further

o Experiment with different blocks in the design section and see how they affect the design of the page.

Themes -
Your Personal Designer

Structure Bot

In this chapter, we will discuss the following topics:

◆ Understanding themes

◆ Exploring various themes

◆ Choosing the perfect theme

◆ Activating the theme on our website

*B*y now, you must have gotten pretty comfortable with WordPress. So you can now:

- Use various options on the dashboard

- Set up your website and its branding

- Manage users and monitor their activity

- Create both dynamic and static content on the website

- Categorize posts using categories and tags

We have covered a lot in our journey so far. Now, we will take a leap and explore a very interesting topic in this chapter. We have an intuitive sense of how things work on WordPress, but we haven't yet tried to design our website until now. We, of course, have formatted our posts and pages by changing color or size, but such design changes have a very localized effect. This means that such formatting affects only that post/page and not any other part of the website.

Themes, on the other hand, are capable of changing the look and feel of the entire website. Thus, by merely clicking a few buttons, we will be able to transform our website.

Understanding themes

Do you remember the house example we discussed in *Chapter 1, WordPress and Subway – Understanding WordPress with the Help of Sandwiches*? Let us go back to that house example but rather in a different way and in context with WordPress.

We will use this house example to recap all we have learned so far and also understand the themes using it.

In this analogy, we will imagine the house to be our website. Someone would require our address to visit our house. The address is the URL in the case of the website. With a URL, anyone can visit our website.

The land on which our house has been built becomes the server. Just as the house resides on the land on which it is built, our website resides in the server. In the case of a WordPress website, this server is also managed by WordPress so that we don't have to worry about it.

Once someone walks into our house, they may see different kinds of things, such as our furniture, electronics equipment, book collection, crockeries, and more. That is just like when someone opens a website and goes through the content on it. Few static furniture stays in the home for many years, such as beds, whereas other items are more dynamic in nature like our electronics equipment. On our website, the static content becomes pages, whereas the dynamic content becomes posts.

But the thing that impresses a guest the most is the design of a house. What does the wall painting color look like? Where is the furniture placed? Does the house have a specific theme like European or maybe a minimalist one? Let us look at a couple of home design examples.

Here is a Victorian theme home design:

Figure 9.1: *Home with Victorian theme*

And here is a house with a Modern theme:

Figure 9.2: *Modern design home*

Do you see how drastically the look and feel of a house changes by its design? The same happens with a website. Just like a house can have a theme, a website can have a theme too. And as you change the theme, the look and feel of the website will change completely.

Different themes will portray posts and pages differently, too. This is again just like how you may differently position your furniture based on the theme of your home.

To recap the analogy we discussed, let's list it down:

- Address of your house –> This is the URL of the website
- Land on which the house is built –> This is the server on which the website is hosted
- House itself –> This is the website
- Furniture and other items of the house –> This is the content on the website (Posts & Pages)
- Design of the house –> This is the Theme on the WordPress website

Choosing a theme

WordPress comes with many themes that you can use to design your website. It is your personal designer on WordPress. For example, if you are building an e-commerce website, then you can choose an e-commerce theme that best matches your requirement. There are quite a few options.

To choose a theme, hover over **Appearance** on the sidebar menu in your dashboard and click on "**Themes**". You will find a lot of different themes as shown in the following screenshot:

Figure 9.3: Recommended themes

You can see that we have a Hever theme installed on our website right now. You may see a different theme, but whichever it is, it will be shown as the Current Theme.

The themes in this list are the recommended ones. If you want to see the complete list of themes, scroll to the bottom and click on the "**Show all themes**" button as in this image:

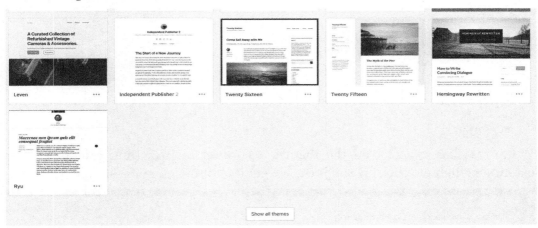

Figure 9.4: *"Show all themes" button*

On Clicking the "**Show all themes**" button, you will be able to see an exhaustive list of themes from various categories, as shown in the following screenshot:

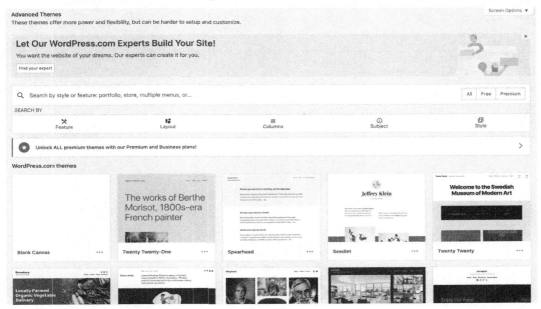

Figure 9.5: *Exploring all themes*

You can now search themes by using the search box. Also, as we are not planning to spend anything, you can click on the **Free** button on the right side of the search box while searching to get only Free themes.

If you are confused about what to search exactly, you can also select one of the options from the "**Search by**" section just below the search box:

- Feature
- Layout
- Columns
- Subject
- Style

WordPress has categorized the themes according to preceding categories. For example, when we click on **Subject**, we get the following suggestions:

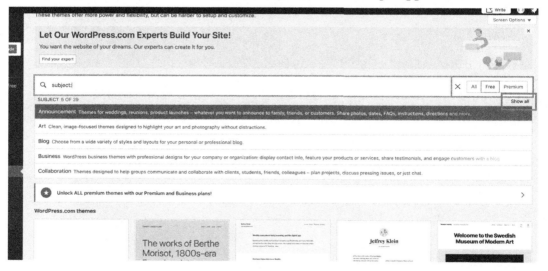

Figure 9.6: Suggestions for the subject category

WordPress is showing 5 suggestions out of 29 for the search category. To check all the search options, click on "**Show All**" as highlighted in the red box in *Figure 9.6*. You will get more search options, as shown in the following figure:

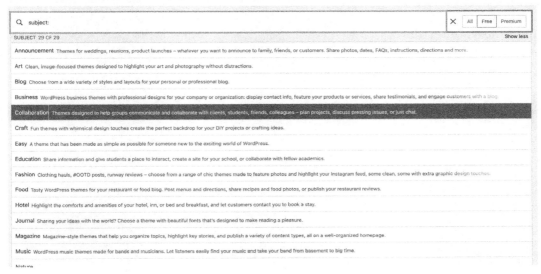

Figure 9.7: Different suggestions for the subject category

You can use these suggestions to choose a subject that may be closely related to your website.

And when we click on **Style**, we get the following suggestions:

Figure 9.8: Different suggestions for style category

If you are looking for a specific style option, like a colorful website or a dark theme website, you can select them from the style suggestions.

As we are building a website around this book and WordPress, which falls under the education category, we will select education from the subject category and get the following results:

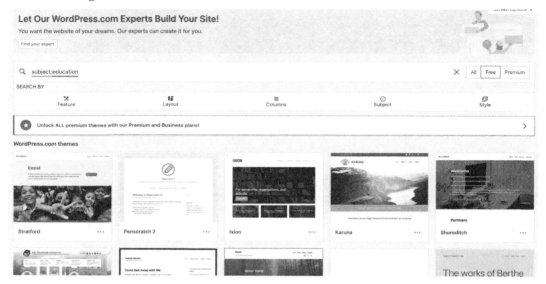

Figure 9.9: Search results for education themes

To get the preview of a theme, you can click on it. You will be taken to the landing page of the theme, which will have all the information about that theme. For most themes, you can also check its live demo. These previews are just like the brochure of the designer who you are hiring to design your home. Before finalizing a designer/decorator for your home, you go through their brochure and then select the most suitable one.

Similarly, you need to have some information about the theme and how it would look on your website before you choose it. This preview will help you with it. For example, I liked the theme "**IXION**", which seemed to match our requirements. Here is how its landing page looked like:

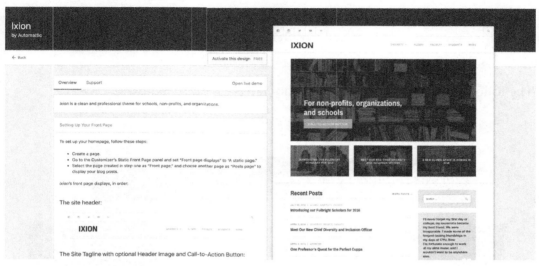

Figure 9.10: *Theme description page*

You can go through the details of the theme on this page. If you want to check its live demo, you can click on the **Open live demo** link, and a preview box will open, which will be similar to the preview box of the post that we saw in *Chapter 6, Creating Your First Post*.

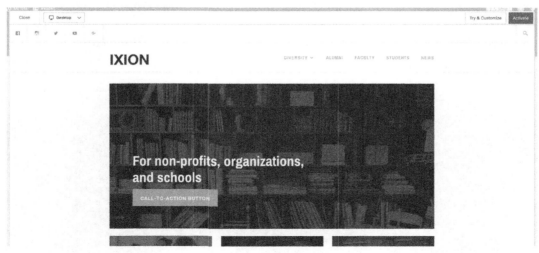

Figure 9.11: *Demo of theme*

If you do not like the theme you opened, you can close this box and go back to the theme page to explore a new theme. But if you like this theme, you can click on the **Activate** button on the top–right corner of this preview box, as shown in *Figure 9.11*.

Once you do that, you will get the option to customize this theme, but you can skip it for now. We will cover customization in the next chapter.

Go ahead and visit your website. Notice the changes.

The following figure shows how our homepage looks like now:

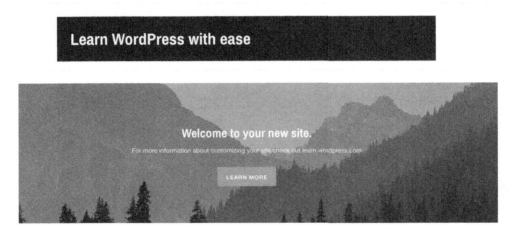

Figure 9.12: *Homepage after activating the new theme*

Compare this with our earlier homepage, which is shown in the following figure:

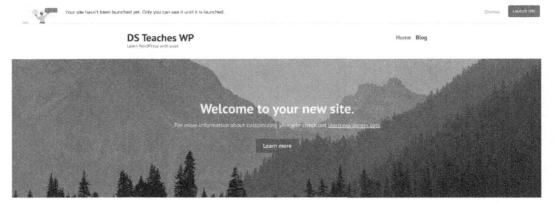

Figure 9.13: *Homepage with the old theme*

The following figure shows how a post appears now:

Figure 9.14: *Post after activating the new theme*

And let us also check out the comment section on a post shown in *Figure 9.15*:

Figure 9.15: *Comment section after activating the new theme*

Compare *Figure 9.14* with *Figure 6.11* and *Figure 9.15* with *Figures 7.1* and *7.2*. Notice the changes in the background color, the font color, font size, font type, and the alignment and spacing of text and boxes. The new theme has minutely changed all the aspects of the look and feel of our website.

And yes, it definitely looks better to me than our previous design. It will look even better once we have configured the theme and customized it in the next chapter.

Themes are going to be an essential tool in your kitty to present your website in the best way possible to your users. And you won't be changing the theme every day. This is so because doing major design changes every now and then will confuse your users. Users generally get used to a design of a website and get comfortable with it. Imagine how would you feel if *Facebook* changed its complete design overnight?

Therefore, you should give some time to select the best theme that matches your requirements. In the next chapter, we will cover how to customize the theme that we select to make it even better for our use case.

Points to Remember

- Making design changes, such as font size or font color, in a post or page has a very localized effect. It only changes the look and feel of that post/page.

- Themes have a major effect on the design of the website as a whole. They change almost every aspect of the website, along with the representation of the post/page.

- In the house and website analogy – house address is the website URL, the land is the server, the house is the website, furniture and other house items is Post/Page, and the design of the house is WordPress Themes.

- There are five categories of themes to simplify your search – Feature, Layout, Columns, Subject, and Style.

- You can check the full details of a theme and even its live demo before activating it on your website.

Multiple Choice Questions

1. Design changes in a Post/Page are also just like changing a theme:
   a. True
   b. False

2. Which one of these is not a category through which you can search themes on WordPress?
   a. Feature
   b. Columns
   c. Rows
   d. Style

3. In the house–website analogy, land on which the house is built is:
   a. Website
   b. Server
   c. URL
   d. None of these

4. Which one of these can you not do by changing the theme?
   a. Change the name of the website
   b. Change how categories are related to posts
   c. Change design of only one post on the website
   d. All of these

Answer Key

1. b   2. c   3. b   4. d

Take it Further

o   Try experimenting with as many themes as possible. Then activate it on your website too, and notice how the website changes.

Chapter 10

Customizing Your Theme

Structure Bot

In this chapter, we will discuss the following topics:

◆ Using the customize option

◆ Revisiting branding settings

◆ Creating a different layout for static pages

In the last chapter, we covered how we can change the design of the whole website using themes. But no matter how carefully you select a theme as per your requirements, you would still want to customize a few aspects of it. In this chapter, we will learn how to customize the theme that we activated on our website in the last chapter.

Objective Bot

At the end of this chapter, you can:

◆ Customize the theme that you activate on your website

◆ Make changes to your theme so that it matches your requirements and branding even better

Using the customize option

To customize the theme you activated on your website in the last chapter, hover over **Appearance** on your sidebar menu and click on **Customize**. When you do

that, a new page will open with a lot of customization options on the left sidebar, as shown in the following figure:

Figure 10.1: Customization options

Let us click on the first customization option: **Site Identity**, as shown in the following figure:

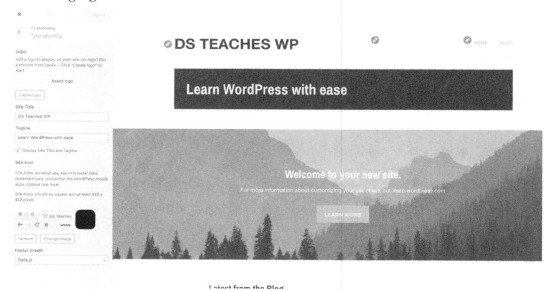

Figure 10.2: Site identity

Revisiting branding settings

In *Chapter 3, Setting Up Your Site*, we had already configured these branding settings. We can change these settings from the Customize theme page too. So go ahead and change the **Site Title**, **Tagline**, and **Logo** if you want to. In the case of the website we are making in this book, we have decided to remove the **Site Title** and **Site Tagline** from their respective places and add only logo.

So, we have uploaded the logo and unchecked the "**Display Site Title and Tagline**" option. We will later add the description of the site at other places and keep this space free. You will have to make such decisions for your website design by considering different pros and cons.

It is not really required to remove Site title and tagline even if you don't want them to appear on your header. Unchecking "Display Site Title and Tagline" checkbox will remove the title and tagline even though if it is present there. This is useful because you may not show it on your header, but websites like Google may still be able to fetch it and show it to their users so that they get an idea what your website is about. That still remains the title of your site, you only chose it to not show on your header for design purposes.

Once you are done making changes, click on the **Save Changes** button on top in your left sidebar, as shown in the following figure:

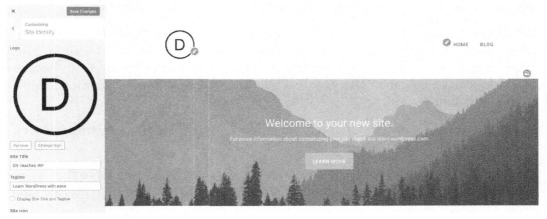

Figure 10.3: Saving the changes

Choosing a color palette for your website

Now, let us click on the back arrow button below the cross button on the top left and come back to different customization options. Then click on **Colors & Backgrounds**. You will now be able to see the options as follows:

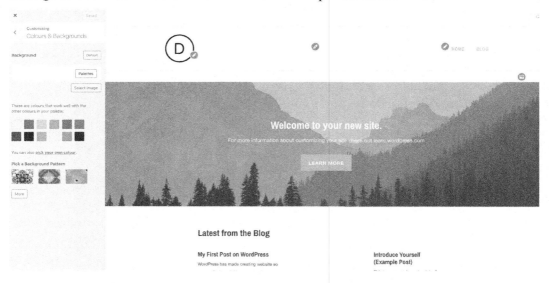

Figure 10.4: Choosing colors

Here you have a few settings that will help you select colors for background, font, buttons, and more throughout your website. Palettes are a combination of colors that will at once configure colors of all elements on your website. WordPress team has carefully created few palettes of colors that go well with each other.

Let us understand this with an example. Suppose you set the background color of your website as black. And then you select the font color as black too. Then obviously, your readers won't be able to read the text on your website because black on top of black won't be visible. Therefore, Palettes contain a combination of such colors that go well with each other.

You also have the option to manually configure your colors by selecting one from various color options.

We will select a Palette from the available options by clicking on **Palette**. As the WordPress team has carefully created these collections using their expertise, that would be recommended.

We have selected a color Palette, and this is how it looks. If you want to check out more Palettes, you can click on the **More** button, as shown in the following figure:

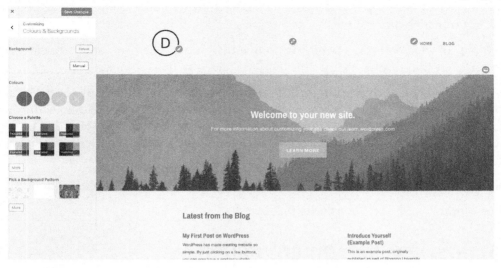

Figure 10.5: Website after selecting a color palette

After changing the color Palette, make sure you save the changes and then go back. Let us explore the next option now, which is Fonts.

Setting font for your website

Fonts is used for setting the font type of different texts throughout our website. On coming to the **Fonts** page, you can see a sidebar as shown in the following figure:

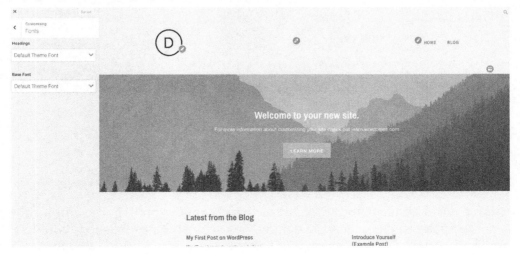

Figure 10.6: Setting fonts

There are two options to change: **Headings** and **Base Font**. Selecting a heading font will change the font of headings throughout your website, such as your page headings, post headings, and so on. The base font will change the font of all other text on your website.

We have selected **Roboto** font for both headings and base font, and you can select one for each you like.

Go back to the Customization option after you have updated your font. The next option is the header image. If you want to add an image to your header section, add an image or select one from WordPress suggestions. WordPress will also provide you a prompt about the dimension of the image that will go well with your theme. We will skip the header image for this website.

The next option is "**Menus**", which we will cover in the next chapter in detail.

After Menus, we have "**Content Options**".

Configuring the content options

Here, we have various options regarding the content on the website, specifically the Posts, as shown in the following figure:

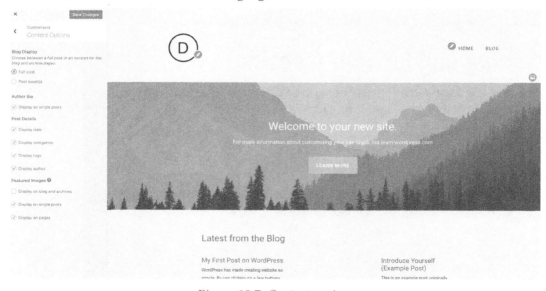

Figure 10.7: Content options

You can control what attributes of a Post should appear on it. For example, if you untick "**Display Date**", then the date when the post was published wouldn't be shown to the user. Similarly, you can also control how the featured image of a Post should be shown. You can control whether a Post in the list of blogs should be shown with a featured image or not.

Try to tick and untick all these options and see how the change happens on your website. Then keep the options that you feel are most suitable for your web visitors.

The next option is **Widgets**, which we will again cover later in this book.

Let us come to the "**Homepage Settings**" option now.

Choosing pages for static content

We can define which page on our website will be the homepage and which page will be the Posts (listing of posts) page. You can see how these options come up in *Figure 10.8*:

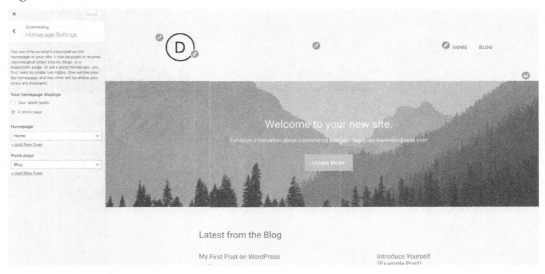

Figure 10.8: Selecting pages

From the Pages that you have created on your website, you can select one page as the homepage. Your theme comes with a default homepage. But you can create one for yourself and make it your homepage.

Similarly, we have selected our **Blog** page as a **Posts** page. The blog page also comes along with the theme that we selected. But you can create a new page for both these pages using what we learned in *Chapter 8, Creating a Page*, and assign them to the **Homepage** or **Posts** page. The theme that you select may or may not come with these two default pages so that you can create them. In any case, the choice is yours.

The next customization option on the list is "**Featured Content**".

Showing your website's featured content

Here, you have the option to add a tag which, when added to any post on your website, will come as a featured post. The theme that we selected has a space for showing featured content. And when we define a tag here, let's say "featured", and if we add it to any post, then that post will come in the space reserved for featured posts. You can see the box for adding the tag name in *Figure 10.9*:

Figure 10.9: *Featured content*

For demonstration purposes, let's add the tag "**wordpress**" here (as shown in *Figure 10.10*) and see what happens. We had already added this tag in the post that we edited in *Chapter 7, Comments, Categories, and Tags*:

Figure 10.10: *Adding tag for the featured section*

Can you see how the Post – "**MY FIRST POST ON WORDPRESS**" comes up on the right below the header? This is so because that is the space our theme has reserved for featured posts. However, we didn't really like this much, so we are skipping this by leaving the tag field empty.

But if you like it or it is presented more beautifully in your theme, you can definitely go ahead with it. You can do so by adding a tag called "featured" here and then adding it to all Posts, which you want to appear in the featured section. This theme supports 3 posts in the featured section as prompted by WordPress, and your theme might support more or less.

You also have the option to select whether the tags of a Post should be shown on a Post or not. We are keeping it visible, but you can select that option if you want to remove it.

Other options

Next up on the customization page, we have three more options:

o **Testimonials:** We will skip this section because we are all launching our website for the first time, so we may not have testimonials to show. Also, there is a chance that all themes might not support it. But you can always come later and try to experiment with this option.

o **Theme Options:** This can be used to add a button or design changes to special features of your theme according to what your theme supports. This option is very specific to the theme that you select. Hence, you can experiment with this option on your own as it will be different for you from what it is for us.

o **Additional CSS:** It is an advanced topic where we can write CSS, which basically is the code via which elements on a website are designed. This is also not available on the free WordPress plan. As we are building a website using no code in this book, we will skip this option.

Viewing the website

Let us take a look at our homepage now, which is shown in the following figure:

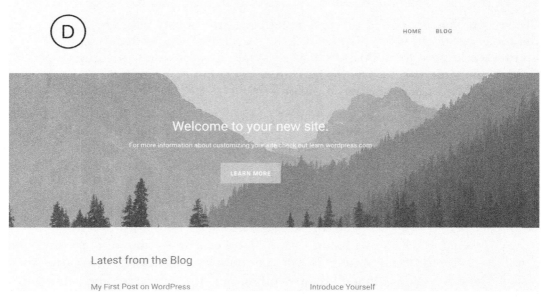

Figure 10.11: Website homepage after design changes

And following is the post page on our website:

Figure 10.12: Post page after design changes

Wow! The website definitely looks much better now than when we started. Let us keep working to make it even better.

In this chapter, we covered various ways to modify the design of our website, and our website now looks much different from when we started. You can experiment with more different options and notice the changes on your website. Your website will look even more beautiful depending upon how much time and effort you give to design and change small elements. So, go ahead and play with the different options we discussed in this chapter and unleash your creative side.

In the next chapter, we will cover Menus in detail, which was also present as a customization option, and see how it can benefit our website users.

- You can choose whether you want to show your site title and tagline or not by checking or unchecking the "Display Site Title and Tagline" option.

- While choosing colors, it is recommended to go for Palettes because they contain a combination of colors that go well with each other.

- There are two types of fonts to change: Headings and Base Font. The heading font will change the font of headings throughout your website and the base font will change the font of all other text.

- Use content options to show/hide or format few details of a post, such as its published date and author details.

- You can define a tag for featured posts on your website, and posts with that tag will appear in the featured section of your theme.

Multiple Choice Questions

1. We can add site title and tagline and still not show it on our website header:
    a. True
    b. False

2. Font for headings and normal text needs to be the same across the website:
    a. True
    b. False

3. Palettes are recommended in this chapter for choosing colors because:
    a. It is easier
    b. It contains a combination of colors that go well with each other
    c. Your website will otherwise not open
    d. All of these

4. The number of posts that comes up in your featured section is:
    a. 3
    b. Depends on the theme you have selected
    c. As many as you want
    d. None of these

Answer Key

1. a   2. b   3. b   4. b

Take it Further

o   Try to experiment with multiple different settings in different options in the Customize section, and notice the changes in your website design.

Chapter 11

Menus - The Map of Your Website

Structure Bot

In this chapter, we will discuss the following topics:

◆ Understanding menus

◆ Different types of menus

◆ Adding menus to your website

*H*ave you read those treasure map stories? In such stories, the main protagonist comes across a map that may lead to the treasure. But the tricky part is that these maps are often difficult to understand and are very cryptic. The main hero would try every possible move in the story and eventually find the treasure using the map (refer to *Figure 11.1*):

Figure 11.1: *A treasure map*

When users are coming to your website, they too would often be looking for something specific. In the case of an e-commerce website, it may be a mobile phone that they are looking for. In this instance, the thing that they would be looking for would be their treasure. And as with treasure map stories, they would need a way to find it.

The menus become the map for your users to find what they are looking for. But you cannot make your maps very difficult to read, as in the treasure map stories. Else your visitors may go away to another website. So we need to provide them a menu that helps them easily navigate our website and find the treasure they are looking for!

Menus are an essential part of a website to make it user-friendly. In this chapter, we will understand their importance.

At the end of this chapter, you will:

◆ Be able to create our own menus on our WordPress website. This will make it easier for our visitors to navigate our website.

Understanding menus

Menus are very important for navigating a website. In *Chapter 4, Few Website Terminologies*, we had already covered a basic definition of the menu and even saw it on the *Amazon* website. Here is the menu of *Amazon*, which we saw in that chapter:

Figure 11.2: Menu on the Amazon website

You can see the menu on the *Amazon* website highlighted in the red box. And the following is the sidebar menu, which we saw in that chapter:

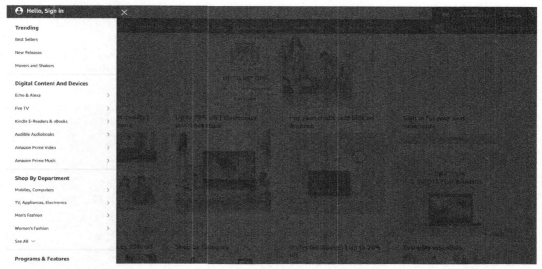

Figure 11.3: *Sidebar Menu on the Amazon website*

Generally, items in menus point to the major pages of your website. For a big website, it is not possible to show all the content on its homepage. So, how will the user know where to go on the website to find the thing he/she is looking for? They can't possibly know all the URLs of that website. This is where menus help.

Different types of menus

In *Chapter 4, Few Website Terminologies*, we had covered two types of menus on the *Amazon* website. In *Figure 11.2*, we can see the normal menu in its header, whereas in *Figure 11.3*, we can see its sidebar menu.

Depending upon how the menus appear at different places on the website, they can be named differently. Generally, the most important menu is the one that a user can directly see on a website. For example, on the Amazon website, as shown in *Figure 11.2*. Amazon has listed the most visited links in this menu.

As most users will be looking for an option from that menu, they would be able to find it there. And hence, it has the most important place on the website. Hence, these kinds of menus are often called *"Primary Menu"*.

But there might be a few users looking for something else. And that is why in *Figure 11.3*, we can see Amazon also has a sidebar menu that lists almost all the important categories from the website in detail. Such menus can be named differently, sometimes they are called *"Secondary Menu"*, sometimes simply a *"Sidebar Menu"*. If there is no menu in the header of the website, then they may as well be called the *"Primary Menu"*.

Apart from these two places, menus can appear at other places too and they would be named accordingly. For example, here is an image of the footer area of the WordPress landing page or homepage:

Figure 11.4: *Footer Menu on WordPress homepage*

You can see many links here in the footer area too. This type of menu, as you may have guessed it, is called *"Footer Menu"*. Many websites use the footer menu to list links of different website sections that they may not have added to their header menu.

The footer comes at last, so it is a great place to add all the links of pages, which may not be frequently visited by most users. That way, we are not adding these to a place where the most important links go. And at the same time, by adding them here, we ensure that those few users who may want to visit these pages would be able to find them.

As we can see, menus can be of different types and it depends upon the area where they appear. Their name also depends on how important a menu is in comparison with other menus on the website. The importance is relative and depends on how easily the user can see it. The header is the top area of the website and the first thing a user sees when they open it. Header menus are generally the most important ones. And that is why they are often called *"Primary Menu"*.

Adding menus to your website

To add a menu to our website, let us again go back to the Customize section, which we covered in the last chapter. Let us select the **Menus** option there this time, as shown in the following figure:

Figure 11.5: *Menus option in Customize section*

Adding the primary menu

You can see that as we discussed, the menu on our header is mentioned here as the primary menu. Let us click on that.

Figure 11.6: *Options for setting Primary Menu*

Reordering the menu

You can make all kinds of changes to your primary menu from here. You can reorder how they appear, or you can add new items to your menu. To reorder how the options are shown in this menu, click on **Reorder**, and then every menu item will have an up and down arrow, which you can use to change their order. Clicking on the up arrow will push it one place above, and clicking on the down arrow will push it one place down. Once you have reordered it, click on **Done**, as shown in the following figure:

Figure 11.7: Reordering option

For example, this is how our website looks in preview if we reorder **BLOG** to make it appear before **HOME**:

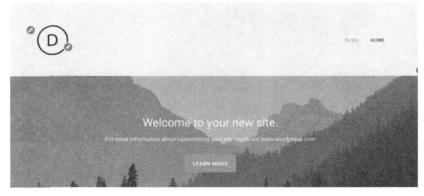

Figure 11.8: Reordered items preview

You can see that **BLOG** comes before **HOME** now.

Adding a new item

Let us add a new item to the menu now. To add a new item, click on the **+ Add Items** button from *Figure 11.6*:

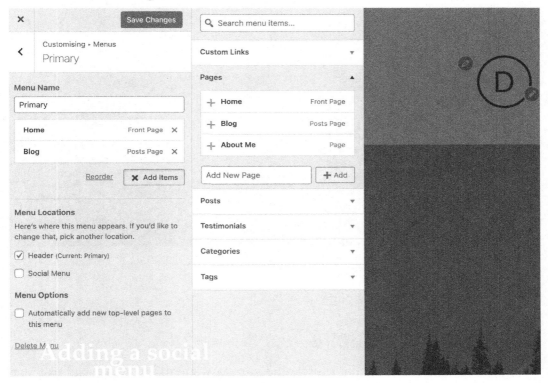

Figure 11.9: *Add a new item to the Menu*

You have the option to show any of your **Page**, **Post**, **Category**, or **Tags** in the menu. Any content that we have created so far in this book can be added as a menu item. But remember, as it is our primary menu and it appears in our header, there are only so many items that we can add there. It is meant only for our website's most important static pages that are most useful for users to navigate our website.

By that logic, let us add our "**About Me**" page earlier that we created in this menu. This is definitely an important page as the website visitors would want to know more about the person who created it. To add the page, click on "**About Me**" and then click on **x Add Items** to close the box of adding new items.

After adding the **About Me** page, it will automatically come after **Blog**, but if you want to reorder it, you can use the reorder option. To save your changes, click on the "**Save Changes**" button. This is how our website looks after adding a new item to this menu:

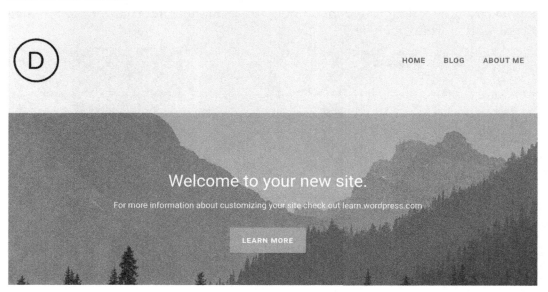

Figure 11.10: *Preview after adding a new Menu item*

Let us go back to the menus page now.

Adding a social menu

In *Figure 11.5*, we can see that our theme supports menus in two locations. The number of menus may be different for other themes. Let us click on **View All Locations** shown in *Figure 11.5* to see the other places where we can add our menu:

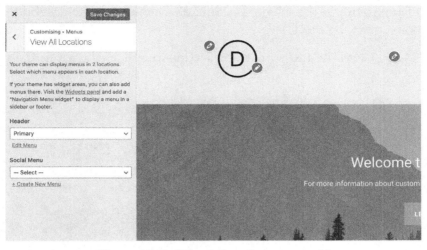

Figure 11.11: Other Menu that we can add

The other menu that we can add is a **Social Menu**, which can point our users to our social media profiles on Facebook, Instagram, or other websites.

Creating a menu

We haven't yet created a **Social Menu**, so to add it click on **Create New Menu** below the **Social Menu** select box, as shown here:

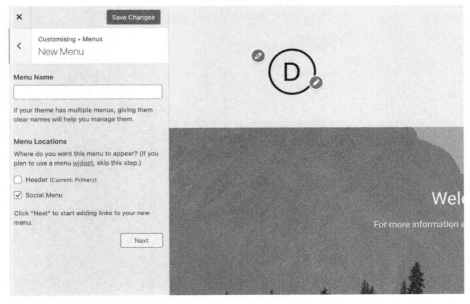

Figure 11.12: Creating a Menu

Let us add the name of the Menu as "**Social Menu**", and select the location as **Social Menu**. Click on **Next**.

Click on **+Add Items** to add something to this menu, as shown in the following figure:

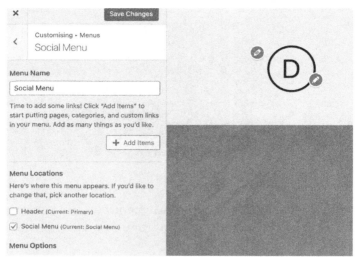

Figure 11.13: Social Menu

As our social media profile links are not part of **Pages**, **Posts**, **Categories**, or **Tags**, we will click on **Custom Links**, which will enable us to add links of other websites, as shown in the following figure:

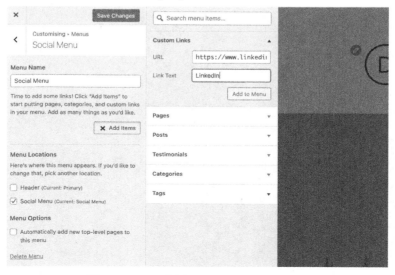

Figure 11.14: Adding a Social Media link

Here, I have added my *LinkedIn* profile, *Facebook* profile, and Medium Profile using this option. You can enter the full URL in the **URL** box and enter the name of the website in **Link Text** and click on the **Add to Menu** button. When you are done adding all your Social Media profiles, click on **Save Changes**. You can see the **Save Changes** button on top in the following figure:

Figure 11.15: *After adding different social media profiles as items*

Let us check this menu on our website. First, you can check the social media links with their icons in the top left (highlighted in red box), as shown in the following figure:

Figure 11.16: *Preview of Menu on website*

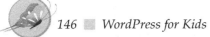

Please note here that even though the social menu appears before our primary menu, it would still be considered as the secondary menu. The reason is that it is not the most easily accessible one, and hence does not contain the most important link for the users. The primary menu, which even though appears after it, is the first menu that grabs the user's attention because of its sizing and placement.

We understood menus extensively in this chapter and also learned how to add it to our WordPress website. Menus are an important part of a website and are crucial to providing a smooth experience to your website visitors. This is why you should spend time on setting it properly.

Until now, we have only used the features provided to us by our theme. In the next chapter, we will cover Widgets, which will help us enhance our theme by adding extra functionalities.

- Items in menus point to the major pages of your website.

- Primary menu is the most important menu on your website and is generally added in the header section.

- Menus can be of different types and it depends upon the area where they appear. Their name also depends on how important a menu is in comparison with other menus on the website.

- Menu can be added to our website from the customize option in appearances on your WordPress sidebar.

- Menus that you can add in different areas depends upon the theme you are using.

- Appearance of your menu will change on different devices according to the responsiveness of your theme.

Multiple Choice Questions

1. **Can there be a website without a menu?**

   a.   Yes

   b.   No

2. **Why are menus used?**

   a.   It makes it very easy for users to visit different pages of website

   b.   A website will not work without a menu

   c.   It looks beautiful

   d.   All of these

3. **What is the difference between the primary menu and the secondary menu?**

   a.   Primary Menu comes before Secondary Menu on the page

   b.   The difference is only in the name

   c.   Primary is more important than Secondary and would be most easily accessible to users

   d.   None of these

Answer Key

1. a   2. a   3. c

Take it Further

o   Visit different websites and check their menus. Identify their Primary and Secondary Menu on the basis of what you have learned in this chapter.

Being Widgety with WordPress

In this chapter, we will discuss the following topics:

◆ Understanding widgets

◆ Different types of widgets

◆ Adding widgets

*W*e have now covered almost all the important options on WordPress to make our website look beautiful. But what if we want to add something of our own imagination to our website?

Currently, we have only added those things to our website, which our theme or WordPress provided by default. It is now time to let our imagination run free. And we can start doing so with the help of **widgets**.

Widgets allow us to add a certain functionality or feature to our website, which otherwise wasn't available. In this chapter, we will cover them in detail, check out different kinds of widgets, and add them to our website.

At the end of this chapter, you will:

◆ Have an understanding of how to extend the functionality of your theme by using widgets

◆ Be able to add a new feature or function to your WordPress website using widgets

Understanding widgets

Let us understand widgets with the help of bicycles. When you purchase a new bicycle, you generally only get the bicycle and not any accessories, such as a mudguard, carriers, water bottle holder, stand, and others. For example, you can see a bare bicycle in the following figure:

Figure 12.1: A bicycle

Your bicycle solves the purpose of riding. You can ride it and go wherever you want. But often we would want some of the accessories to enhance the cycle ride experience. And so, we would get a few accessories, which we may require.

Similarly, by using default WordPress options, we are able to create a website that loads with content. But again, we may want to add a few enhancements to our website as we seem fit. This can be achieved with the help of widgets on WordPress.

Like you have mudguard, stand, bottle holder, and other feature enhancements for your bicycle, WordPress provides widgets like text block, search field, list of authors, and others that you can show on your website. You can check some of the available widgets in WordPress in *Figure 12.2*:

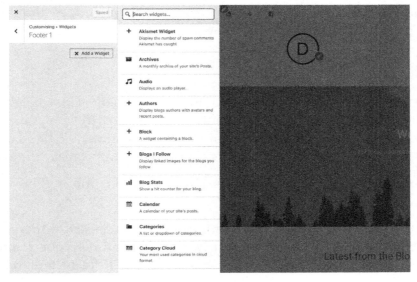

Figure 12.2: *Available widgets*

Although bicycles can be enhanced with different accessories, most of them can be added to only those places where the bicycles support it. For example, most bicycles come with a slot for water bottle holder, and so such holders can only be put up there. Similarly, there are many available widgets that you can use to add custom content to the design of your website. But these widgets can only be added to those places where your theme supports it.

In our current theme, the places shown in *Figure 12.3* are available where we can add widgets:

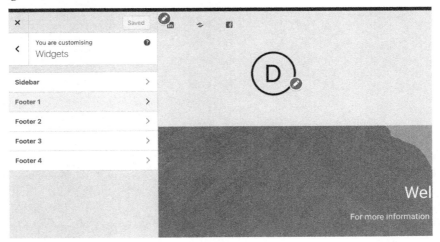

Figure 12.3: *Different widget areas*

This means that we can add any widget from the list of widgets that WordPress provides in the slots available in our theme.

Adding a widget

To add a widget, open the **Widgets** section on the Customise page. Let us add a few custom widgets to our footer section. As you can see, the footer in our theme has been divided into 4 sections, which means 4 columns. We had covered the concept of columns in *Chapter 8, Creating a Page*, when we were creating pages.

Select **Footer 1** and click on the **Add a Widget** button. You will be able to see different widgets as shown in *Figure 12.2*.

We already have an **About Me** page. But it would make sense to add a small piece of content about the website in the footer too. This will help our visitors know about the website on every page without visiting a specific page for it. If they want to know more, then they can visit the About Me page.

To add a piece of text there, let us select the **Text** widget, as shown in the following figure:

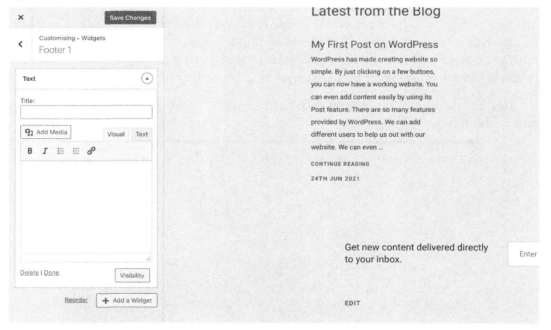

Figure 12.4: Adding a text widget

Enter your content and click on **Save Changes**. You can see how the content comes up on the website in *Figure 12.5*:

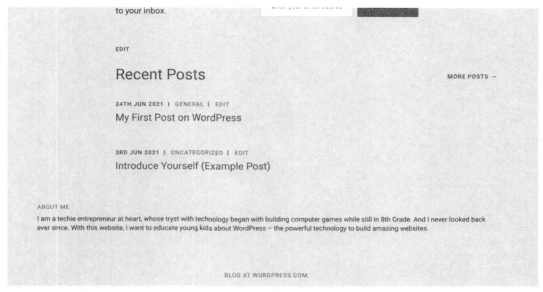

Figure 12.5: Preview of content added in the text widget

Currently, this text is taking up the whole space of footer. As we had seen before, our theme supports 4 widgets in 4 different columns of the footer. So, when we add more widgets in other footers, this text will auto-adjust its width. But we will only be able to add a maximum of 4 different footers in 4 columns.

You can also add multiple widgets in the same footer column. Let us go ahead and also add our social media icons in **Footer 1**. To do so, again click on **Add a Widget** and select **Social Icons**.

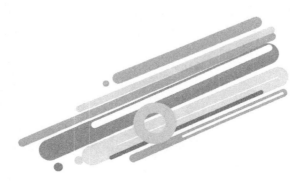

You can add a **Title** and different links to your social media profiles, as shown in *Figure 12.6*:

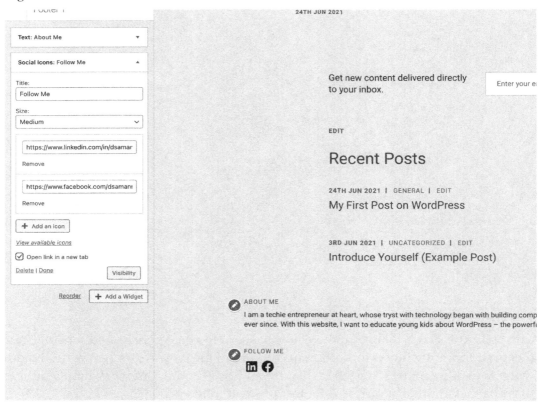

Figure 12.6: *Social Icons widget*

When you have added the social media links, click on **Save Changes**. Let us add a widget in **Footer 2** now.

In footer 2, we would like to add a **Monthly Archive** of our posts as shown in *Figure 12.7*. This would allow our visitors to check out posts, which were published in a particular month. With technologies like WordPress, new updates keep coming, and being able to view posts by month may be useful for our visitors:

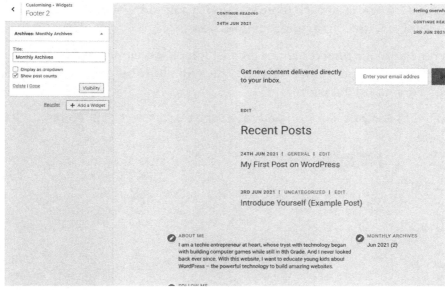

Figure 12.7: *Archives widget*

As we keep adding new posts in new months, those months will also keep coming here.

Let us now add a Search box in **Footer 3**, as shown in the following figure. This will allow our visitors to search posts or any content on our website using this search box. When our visitors may not be able to find what they are looking for, this search feature can help them:

Figure 12.8: *Search widget*

Do note how the width of each footer section is auto-adjusting on its own whenever we are adding a widget to a new footer section.

We will now add our final footer. In the last footer, we would like to add the link to the top posts and pages on the website. This will allow our users to navigate to the most read content on the website.

To do so, go to **Footer 4**, click on `Add a Widget` and select `Top Posts & Pages`, as shown here:

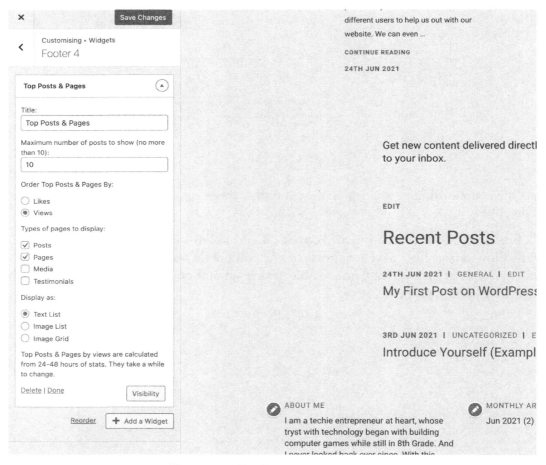

Figure 12.9: Top Posts & Pages widget

You can select the options you want, whether you want to show only posts or both Posts & Pages, or you want to order top content according to likes or views. Feel free to experiment with different selections.

After you are done, click on **Save Changes**.

Now, our final complete footer on the website looks like this:

Figure 12.10: *Preview of widgets added to the footer area*

Did you see how you had complete freedom to add any kind of widgets in these areas, which were supported by our theme? The theme that you select might provide some other areas too where you can add widgets to your website. For example, the theme on this website also has the option of adding a sidebar widget. So, feel free to check out the supported areas of your theme.

Now that we understand widgets, go ahead and start adding them to different areas of your website. Also, experiment with different widgets. In this chapter, we covered 5 different types of widgets, but there are many more widgets that you can explore. Figure out what would be most helpful for your website visitors and add them.

In the next chapter, we will explore the Premium options of WordPress. We will also understand the benefits of switching to their premium plan and how it is done.

Points to Remember

- WordPress widgets are like bicycle accessories. As your bicycle accessories help you enhance your riding experience on the bicycle, widgets allow you to enhance your website as per your choice.

- Widgets can only be added to those places that are supported by your theme.

- Text widget allows you to add custom content, whereas social media widget allows you to add your social media links with their icons.

- Search widget allows your users to search content on your website.

- Archive widget shows content categorized by months in which they were published.

- Top Posts & Pages show the top-performing post and pages on your website. You can customize different settings in this widget.

Multiple Choice Questions

1. **Widgets allow you to change the functionality of your theme.**

    a. True

    a. False

2. **You can add multiple widgets in an area of your theme that supports widgets.**

    a. True

    b. False

3. **Which one of these widgets allow you to show sorted content on your website based on the number of likes?**

    a. Search

    b. Top Posts & Pages

    c. Archives

    d. All of these

4. **Which one of these does widget not do?**

    a.   Enable you to add content to a supported widget area

    b.   Change the way you create pages

    c.   Allow you to add your social media links in a supported widget area

    d.   All of these

Answer Key

1. b   2. a   3. b   4. b

Take it Further

o   Find out the widget areas supported by your theme and try experimenting with different widgets in those areas.

Going for a Paid Plan - Is It Required?

Structure Bot

In this chapter, we will discuss the following topics:

- ◆ Understanding paid plans
- ◆ Features that will be available post-upgrade to a paid plan
- ◆ Upgrading to a paid plan
- ◆ Getting a domain for your website

*I*n *Chapter 2, Getting Started – Create Your Account and Start Exploring*, while creating our account, we had an option to purchase a paid plan on WordPress, but we went with the free plan. Now that we have covered the available options for free on WordPress, it is time to look at their paid plans.

Let us explore their different paid plans in this chapter and understand what benefits it can provide us.

Objective Bot

This chapter aims to introduce you to different paid plans on WordPress. At the end of this chapter, you can:

- ◆ Decide for yourself whether you need a paid plan. And if so, you will be able to upgrade to one
- ◆ Purchase a custom domain and connect it to our website.

Understanding premium plans

There are three types of online products (we will call websites as products in this discussion) available these days:

- Free
- Paid
- Freemium

Examples of free products would be *Facebook* or *Google*. *Facebook* or *Google* don't directly charge you anything for using their product. But as a business, they also have to earn money. They do so by showing you ads instead of charging you for using their website.

Paid products are those products for which you have to pay to use them. An example of such a product would be *Netflix*. If you want to watch *Netflix*, you need to pay some money every month.

The third type of products are freemium products, and WordPress falls in that category. With freemium products, it is free to use their basic features. But if you want to use their advanced features, you need to pay them something. This is why till now, we were able to create our website for free; but now, to use a few of their advanced add-on features, we need to switch to a paid plan.

By switching to one of their paid plans, we will use a few extra features. If you remember, in *Chapter 3, Setting Up Your Site*, when we were learning how to check website activity, we were only able to see 20 most recent activities. By upgrading to a paid plan, we will be able to see much more. Wouldn't that be helpful?

Similarly, there are many more features that we will get on upgrading our account to a paid plan. We will cover some of those in this chapter and others in the coming chapters.

Different paid plans

To check out different paid plans, hover over upgrades in your dashboard sidebar menu and click on **Plans**. You will see different plans as shown in *Figure 13.1*:

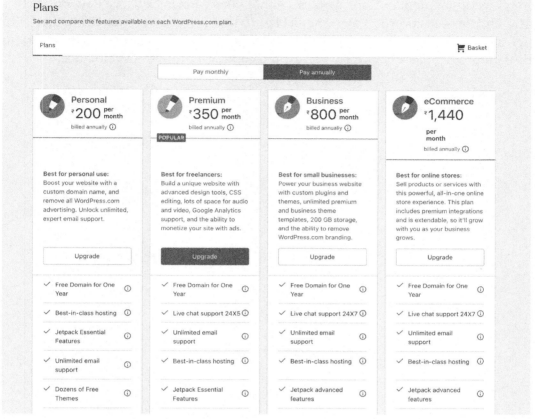

Figure 13.1: *Different paid plans*

You can see four different plans that you can choose from:

- **Personal**: It comes with very basic add-on features and is best for personal use.

- **Premium**: It allows usage of advanced design tools on top of what personal provides. It is best for freelancers who want to build a unique website.

- **Business**: It comes with extra storage, unlimited themes, and plugins on top of what premium provides. This is best for small businesses, which need additional tools. We will go ahead with this plan because we want to explore plugins in this book. It is an extremely powerful feature.

- **eCommerce**: This plan is best for e-commerce websites that require full premium integrations and tools to run their business.

You can read more about what each plan provides in its respective columns.

In terms of payment options, you can either "**Pay annually**" or "**Pay monthly**". The current selection is **Pay annually**. If you select **Pay monthly**, the price per month will increase, as shown in *Figure 13.2*. The idea is to provide an extra discount to people who are paying for the coming 12 months in advance:

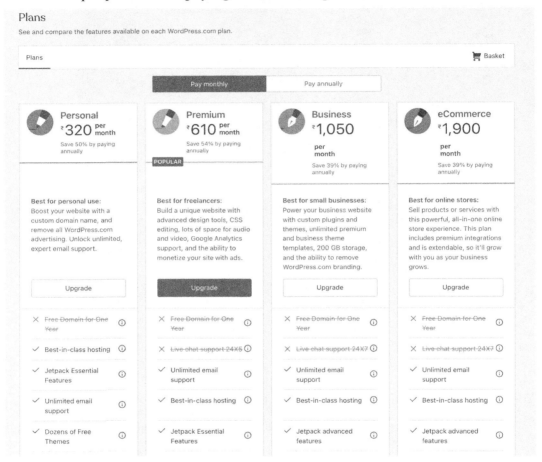

Figure 13.2: *Paid plans with monthly payment option*

Few of the features are also stroked off when you select **Pay monthly** option.

"**Business**" seems to be the perfect choice for us. However, we will suggest you to go ahead with Business too, as the topics that we will cover in the coming chapters won't be available with the **Personal** and **Premium** plan.

For payment options, we will go ahead with the monthly plan. But you may also opt annual payment option as it will provide you extra discount and a free domain for a year. We will purchase the domain separately along with the monthly payment of the "**Business**" plan. However, no matter which payment option or plan you choose, the flow of setting up would remain almost the same as discussed in this chapter.

Completing the purchase

Once you have selected your payment option and finalized a plan for yourself, click on **Upgrade**. Feel free to read other features too that come with each plan. You will be able to understand the meaning of these features better as we progress in the book.

Upon clicking on the **Upgrade** button, you will be taken to the Checkout page, as shown in *Figure 13.3*:

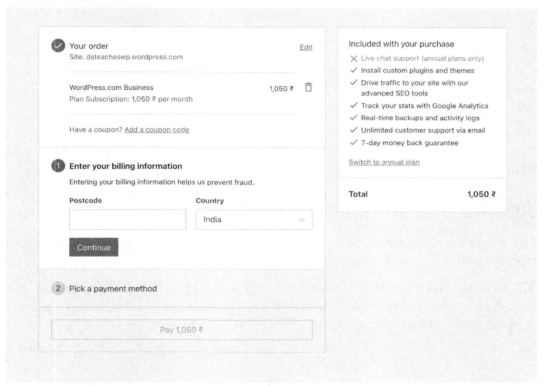

Figure 13.3: Checkout screen

Enter your postcode and click on **Continue**. Post that, with the help of your parents, enter the card details and then click on the **Pay** button.

After your payment is successful, you will get a confirmation page for your payment, as shown here:

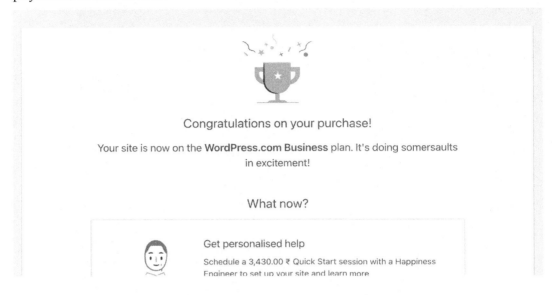

Figure 13.4: Payment success screen

You can close this page after seeing the confirmation message. You will also get an email confirmation for your purchase.

Adding a custom domain

Let us go back to our WordPress dashboard. First, we will purchase a custom domain and link it with our website.

Till now, we have been using a domain with the "*.wordpress.com*" extension. But that does not look very professional. Most of the successful websites have a direct domain with extensions like "*.com*", "*.in*", "*.org*", and so on.

Click on **Domains** by hovering over **Upgrades** in your sidebar menu, and you will get the following page:

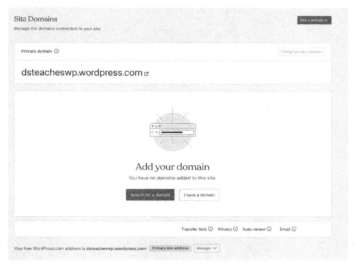

Figure 13.5: *Domain page on the dashboard*

As we want to add a new domain to our website, let us search which domain would be the most suitable. Click on the "**Search for a domain**" button. The interface would be very similar to the one we explored while searching the domain in *Chapter 2, Getting Started – Create Your Account and Start Exploring*.

We won't have to search this time much, though, as luckily, for our case, *dsteacheswp. com* is available, as you can see in the following figure:

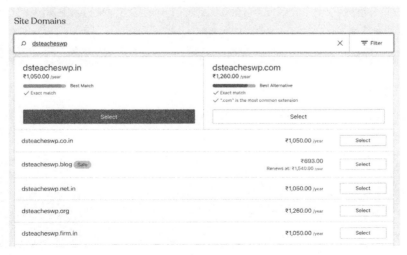

Figure 13.6: *Searching for the domain name*

We will select that option and move ahead. On the next screen, you may be asked to purchase few add-ons like email with your domain. But again, you can skip that and move ahead, as you can always configure those later.

You will get a similar checkout screen, as shown in *Figure 13.3*. You can enter your details there and pay the amount. You will again get a success message and an email after your domain purchase, as shown here:

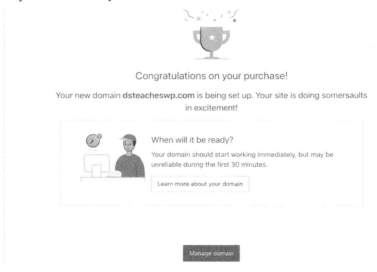

Figure 13.7: Screen after successfully purchasing the domain

Wait for a few minutes after your purchase and then go ahead and open the website by entering your new domain name. Voila! Your website now opens with a professional extension, as shown in *Figure 13.8*. We no longer have to type *".wordpress.com"* in our domain anymore:

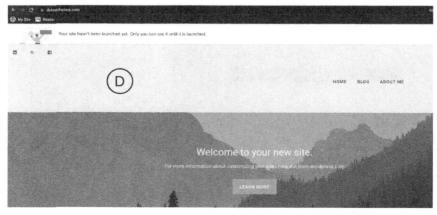

Figure 13.8: Website opening with new custom domain name

Other benefits of upgrading

Do you remember how in *Chapter 3, Setting Up Your Site*, while checking website activity, we were only able to check the 20 most recent activities? Guess what? That restriction would have now faded away.

Let us check the website activity log once again. Hover over Jetpack on your sidebar menu and click on the **Activity Log**, and you can see the following screen:

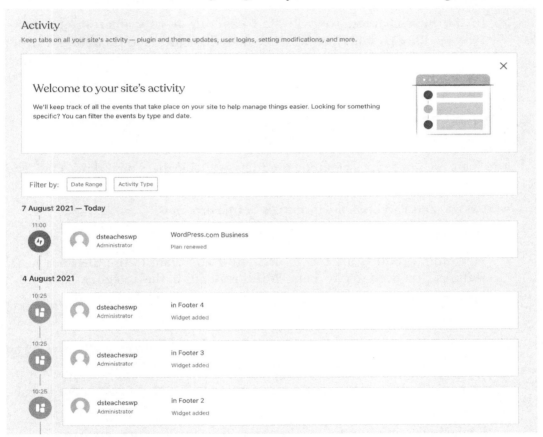

Figure 13.9: *Website activity log page after upgrading to a paid plan*

There is no mention of any restriction now, and you can keep scrolling to find the past activity logs of your website.

Go ahead and find out what more things or sections you can access post upgrading to paid plan on WordPress. There would be quite a few other benefits.

Recap

In this chapter, we covered how we can upgrade our account to one of the paid plans. We then even bought a domain and connected it to our WordPress website.

In the next chapter, we will start covering a very interesting topic – Plugins. Plugins will open a whole new door for us to do a lot of further customization on our website. So get ready to take your website to the next level!

Points to Remember

- There are three types of online products available these days: Free, Paid, and Freemium.

- Google and Facebook are examples of free products.

- Netflix is an example of a paid product.

- Freemium products are free to use, but if you want to use their advanced features, you need to pay them. WordPress falls in this category.

- There are four different paid plans on WordPress – Personal, Premium, Business and eCommerce.

- There are two payment options available – monthly and annually. You get an extra discount if you pay annually in advance for 12 months.

- You can purchase a domain after upgrading to a paid plan, and your website will open with that custom domain.

- It takes a few minutes for the domain to be activated after purchase.

- You can check full website activity logs after upgrading to a paid plan.

Multiple Choice Questions

1. Which one of these is not an example of a Free product?

    a. Google

    b. Instagram

    c. Netflix

    d. Facebook

2. We are now able to see full website activity logs because:

    a. We purchased a custom domain name

    b. We upgraded to a paid plan

    c. Both A and B

    d. None of these

3. Is buying a custom domain mandatory after upgrading to a paid plan?

    a. Yes

    b. No

Answer Key

| 1. | c | 2. | b | 3. | b |

Take it Further

o Try to explore your WordPress dashboard and see which new options are available after upgrading to a paid plan.

Chapter 14

Introducing the Plugins

Structure Bot

In this chapter, we will discuss the following topics:

◆ Understanding plugins

◆ Few use cases of plugins

◆ Searching and adding a plugin

In *Chapter 12, Being Widgety with WordPress*, we covered about widgets. Widgets allowed us to extend the functionality of our theme by adding a few extra features. But those features were limited in number. WordPress provided us a predefined list from which we had to choose.

What if you want to add a completely different feature to your website and extend the functionality of WordPress itself? In this chapter, we will cover plugins that will allow us to do that.

Objective Bot

At the end of this chapter, you will:

◆ Get introduced to plugins, post which, you will understand what plugins are and why we should use them

◆ Also know how to look for a plugin and add it to our WordPress website.

Understanding plugins

Widgets allowed you to add new content blocks or functionality (if you might say so) at designated places in your website.

What if you don't just want to extend the existing functionality of your theme but even add new functionality or feature to it? For example, what if you wanted to add a pop-up to your website? Or a chat option? What can we do then? This is where plugins come to your rescue.

Don't get confused with widgets. With widgets, you could add text, social icons, and so on, which were already provided as a default functionality by WordPress. With plugins, you extend the functionality of WordPress itself. It then allows you to add something completely new, which you couldn't add earlier.

Let us come back to our bicycle example, which we discussed earlier while understanding widgets. Our bare bicycle came with certain slots where we could add new parts to it. But those parts were pretty standard. For example, you could add a water bottle holder in a slot or a stand in its slot.

But if you have a custom requirement, like adding an electric engine to your bicycle, then your bicycle does not come with a default slot for it. You will need someone else to come and do it for you.

Similarly, when our requirements were pretty standard on our website, we made our way with widgets by adding them in their slots. But now, when we have complete custom requirements, plugins will help us out.

If you haven't yet upgraded to a paid plan, you wouldn't be able to follow the instructions in this chapter. Plugins are only available for paid users on WordPress. To upgrade to a paid plan, please refer *Chapter 13, Going For a Paid Plan – Is it required?*

The creators of plugins

The plugins are generally made by other developers or companies who add it to the WordPress plugin repository. As a result, WordPress has a lot of plugins from thousands of developers.

These developers or companies try to understand user requirements, which may not be fulfilled by WordPress's offerings. They then create plugins for it. Users who use these plugins can also review the plugin. As WordPress does not always directly provide these plugins, it is important to know if the plugin is good. And you can know that by reading the reviews of that plugin.

Few use cases for using a plugin

To understand plugins even better, let us cover a few use cases. We had referred to two use cases earlier in this chapter – Adding pop-ups and chat option. Next, we will cover five more use cases in detail, which can be addressed by using plugins:

◆ Adding a contact form: You must have visited many websites where there is a contact page. These contact pages generally have a contact form that the website visitors can use to contact the owner or support team of the website.

◆ Adding sliders: Don't sliders look beautiful? It is also a great way to show beautiful images on your homepage related to your business.

◆ Share buttons: Adding share buttons that allow your website visitors to share your content on social media is a great marketing technique.

◆ Increasing security of your website: Cyber-attacks have become very common nowadays. As your website becomes more popular, there may be instances of someone trying to hack your website. You can use security plugins to secure your website to prevent such cases.

◆ Sending newsletters: Good companies often send out newsletters to their customers by email to inform them about any ongoing offers or new content. You too can do the same on your website using a plugin that enables you to send newsletters to your customers.

Previously mentioned use cases are only a few. There can be many more such cases. It is meant to give you an idea about the uses of plugins. In the coming chapters, we will cover few most popular plugins that solve the most common occurring use cases and understand how to use them.

Searching and adding a plugin

Let us go on the following plugins page by clicking on **Plugins** in the left sidebar menu on the WordPress dashboard:

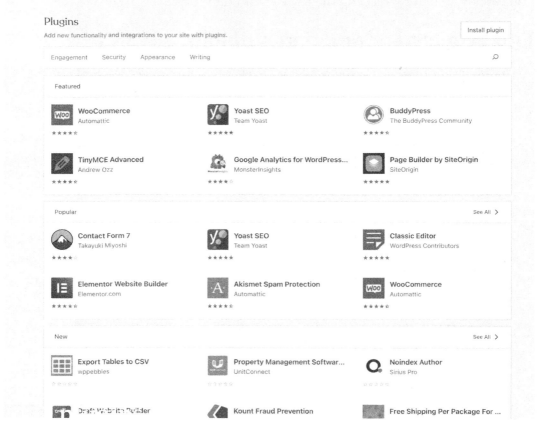

Figure 14.1: List of plugins

You can find many different plugins on this page sorted by different sections. On the top menu, there are different categories like **Engagement**, **Security**, **Appearance**, and **Writing**. To explore plugins in those categories, you can click on them, and you would be able to see plugins only from those categories.

Checking plugins by category

You can check the plugins from the **Engagement** category in *Figure. 14.2*. As you may have guessed it, engagement plugins will help you increase the engagement of your website visitors, as shown in the following figure:

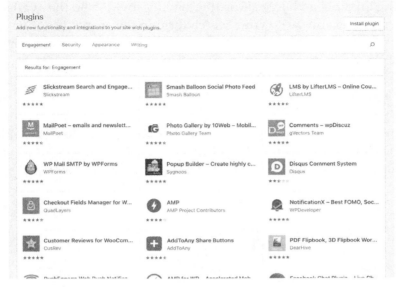

Figure 14.2: Plugins from the engagement category

In *Figure 14.1*, by default, the featured and popular plugins are listed first, followed by new plugins added to the platform. You can explore different plugins as per their category or their popularity.

Searching a plugin

You can also search for plugins. To search a plugin, click on the search icon on the right side of categories, as shown in the following figure:

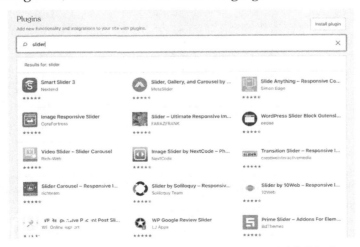

Figure 14.3: Plugins that match search keyword "slider"

After clicking on the search icon, WordPress will provide you the available plugins for that keyword as you write your search term in the search box. For example, in *Figure 14.3*, you can see we typed "`slider`" in the search box and got many results related to sliders.

Installing a plugin

To check the details of a plugin and install it, we will have to click on it. First, let us check the details of a plugin called "*Yoast SEO*" from *Figure 14.1*. It is a very popular plugin, and we will cover it in detail in the next chapter:

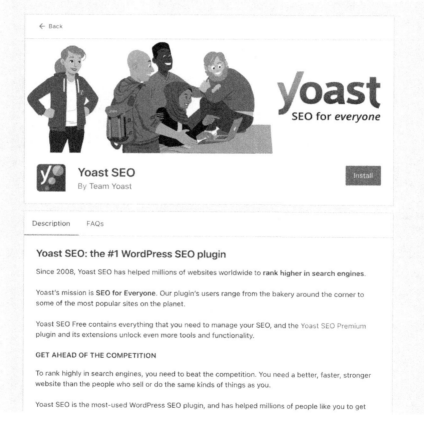

Figure 14.4: *Details of Yoast SEO plugin*

When you click on a plugin, you can see its entire details. You can read about the plugin, check who created the plugin, and a lot more.

We will understand more about this plugin in the next chapter. For now, we will install it. To install the plugin, click on the **Install** button.

The plugin will start installing after you click the install button. It might take a few minutes. While it is installing, you may see a page as shown in *Figure 14.5.*

Figure 14.5: *Installing Yoast SEO plugin*

After the installation is complete, you will receive a success message. You may also be redirected to a setup page, but we can ignore that for now. We will set up this plugin in the next chapter when we cover it in detail.

If you check your WordPress dashboard's sidebar menu, you can now find a new Yoast SEO option there, as shown in the following figure:

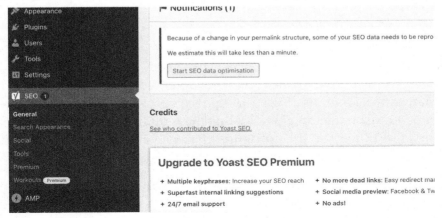

Figure 14.6: *Yoast SEO in your sidebar menu on the dashboard*

You can also check all the installed plugins on your website by clicking on **Installed Plugins** after hovering over **Plugins** in your sidebar menu, as shown here:

Figure 14.7: *List of installed plugins on your website*

Many of the plugins on this page have been installed by default when you upgraded to the paid package. That is so because they are required to provide a few of the options promised to you while upgradation.

Based on what we learned in this chapter, you can go ahead and explore many more plugins. Every plugin comes with its own set of options depending on the functionality that the plugin provides. We will be setting up a few plugins in the upcoming chapters, and you can then see how the setup options change from one plugin to another.

In the next chapter, we will set up the Yoast SEO plugin, which we installed in this chapter. It is a very popular plugin on WordPress, which is used by a majority of websites.

Points to Remember

- With widgets, you could add text, social icons, and so on, which were already provided as a default functionality by WordPress. With plugins, you extend the functionality of WordPress itself.

- Plugins are only available for paid users on WordPress.

- Plugins are generally made by other developers or companies who then add it to the WordPress plugin repository.

- The plugins are not always directly provided by WordPress, so it is important to know if the plugin is good. You can know that by reading the reviews of that plugin.

- You can find plugins by their category, popularity, or even search them using the search icon button.

- To check the details of a plugin and install it, you have to click on a plugin.

- Installation of a plugin may take a few minutes.

- Every plugin comes with its own set of options depending on the feature that the plugin provides.

Multiple Choice Questions

1. **Which one of these can a plugin do?**
   a. Enable you to create pages differently
   b. Add a slider to your website
   c. Add a contact form on your website
   d. All of these

2. **Plugins and widgets are the same:**
   a. True
   b. False

3. **Why should you check the review of a plugin before installing it?**

   a. It is fun to read

   b. To check whether it is a good plugin, as they are made by othercdevelopers

   c. It makes it easy to install a plugin

   d. None of these

4. **Every plugin works the same way and comes with the same options:**

   a. True

   b. False

Answer Key

1. d   2. b   3. b   4. b

Take it Further

o Explore more plugins by category. Also, try searching and installing different types of plugins from your imagination. See how different plugins come with varied options.

Chapter
15

Rank Your Website:
SEO with Plugin

Structure Bot

In this chapter, we will discuss the following topics:

◆ Basics of SEO

◆ Setting up Yoast SEO plugin

◆ Using Yoast SEO plugin

*W*here do you go when you are looking for something on the Internet? Let us suppose you want to know about *WordPress*. What will you do? Most of us would go to *Google*, and enter in the search box *"What is WordPress?"*. Google will then provide us the list of relevant search results, as shown in the following figure:

Figure 15.1: *A person searching on Google*

Apart from the websites that we frequently use, we often rely on Google to take us to a relevant website for our queries. We don't directly type their address in our browser because there are so many websites on the Internet, and we can't know them all. But how does Google decide which websites to show in search results? This is done through **Search Engine Optimization (SEO)**. SEO enables you to get visitors to your website by ranking it in search results.

At the end of this chapter, you will:

◆   Understand the basics of SEO

◆   Learn about the Yoast SEO plugin and also learn how to use it effectively to rank our website in search results

Basics of SEO

SEO stands for Search Engine Optimization. As the name says, it means optimizing your website for search engines.

When we do so, the ranking of our website in Google becomes better. When you search a query on Google, do you go to other pages of the search results? Most of us would only click on one of the top 3-4 links that come up. And that is why getting a good rank on Google is important. An improved ranking would mean more clicks and, therefore, more website visitors.

There are various ways in which SEO can be done, and WordPress automatically takes care of most of those. But there are a few things you can do to ensure better SEO, and we will cover those in this chapter. First, we will cover why we need SEO.

The need for SEO

As a website owner, you definitely want people to come and visit your website. During the initial days, you may ask your friends to check out your website and they may ask their friends. But at some point, you would want people from out of your network to visit your website too. You can do so by running ads on different websites such as *Facebook*. Although, that is a very costly way to get visitors.

Search engines like Google provide you the website visitors for free. And so, it makes sense to get as many visitors from them as possible because you aren't getting charged anything for it.

Also, the visitors from Google are people looking for content that your website is about. That is so because Google will only show them your website when it matches with their search query. Hence, they will engage the most with your website and may even become regular visitors. On the other hand, your friends may or may not be interested in knowing what your website is all about.

Now, you may be wondering why SEO? Isn't it Google's job to provide the best search results to its users? If you are thinking so, you are correct. In fact, Google has become very smart these days. It can rank websites that have good content but may not be most optimized for SEO.

Still, it doesn't hurt to go that extra mile and do something from your end that enables Google to rank your website better. After all, it will provide you only visitors, right? Also, SEO may speed up your ranking, which may otherwise even take many months or years on its own.

We will interchangeably use the words "Search Engines" and "Google" in this chapter. Although, Google is just one of the search engines but it is the most widely used one and hence we will mostly refer to it.

Setting up Yoast SEO plugin

Let us go ahead and set up our Yoast SEO plugin now. We had already installed Yoast SEO plugin in the last chapter. Before we start, make sure that the plugin is activated on your website. To do so, hover over plugins and click on **Installed Plugins** on the WordPress sidebar menu.

Scroll down to find Yoast SEO plugin in the list and if it is deactivated, activate it by clicking on **Activate link** as shown in *Figure 15.2*. You can skip this step if the plugin is already activated:

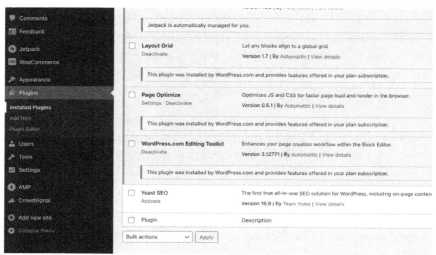

Figure 15.2: Activating the plugin

Once the plugin is activated, hover over SEO in your sidebar menu and click "**General**". You will be taken to the following **General Settings** page of the Yoast SEO plugin:

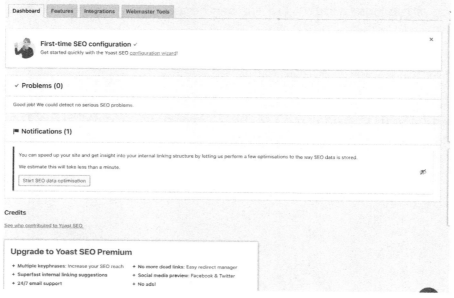

Figure 15.3: General settings

First of all, click on the **Start SEO data optimization** button on this page. On clicking it, Yoast SEO will understand your website and how different links are structured on your website. On the basis of that, it will automatically do a few optimizations that will boost your SEO. Once you are done, you will get a success message, as shown in *Figure 15.4*:

Yoast SEO comes with some very powerful built-in tools:

- **Import and Export**
  Import settings from other SEO plugins and export your settings for re-use on (another) blog.

- **File editor**
  This tool allows you to quickly change important files for your SEO, like your robots.txt and, if you have one, your .htaccess file.

- **Bulk editor**
  This tool allows you to quickly change titles and descriptions of your posts and pages without having to go into the editor for each page.

- **Optimise SEO Data**
  You can speed up your site and get insight into your internal linking structure by letting us perform a few optimisations to the way SEO data is stored. If you have a lot of content, it might take a while, but trust us, it's worth it. Learn more about the benefits of optimised SEO data.

  ✓ SEO data optimization complete

Upgrade to Yoast SEO Premium

+ **Multiple keyphrases:** Increase your SEO reach   + **No more dead links:** Easy redirect manager

+ **Superfast internal linking suggestions**   + **Social media preview:** Facebook & Twitter

+ **24/7 email support**   + **No ads!**

Get Yoast SEO Premium ▶

Figure 15.4: SEO data optimization completion

You can find the button "Get Yoast SEO Premium" as in Figure 15.4 even though we have updated to a paid plan on WordPress. Upgrading to a paid plan on WordPress has now enabled us to install plugin but a few plugins can still charge separately. We had discussed in last chapter that these plugins are generally made by other developers or companies. Charging a certain amount is how these developers or companies make money. However, Yoast SEO plugin is available as a freemium plugin and we will only be using its free features. So, there is no need to upgrade to its premium version.

We will leave the other settings as it is on the **General** settings page. There is no need to change any default setting; however, you can go through them if you want to explore.

Again, hover over SEO on your sidebar menu and now click on **Search Appearance**. Scroll down on that page till you reach the "**Knowledge Graph & Schema.org**" settings option as shown in *Figure 15.5*:

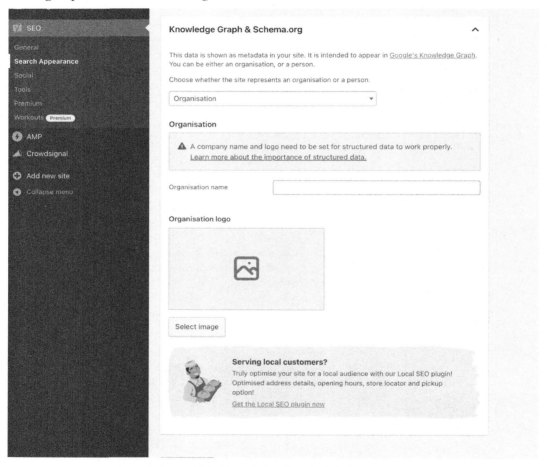

Figure 15.5: Knowledge Graph & Schema.org

This option allows you to let search engines like Google know whether your website represents a person or an organization. For example, if your website is about yourself, then your website represents a person, but if it is for your business then it represents an organization. Select the correct option and then enter the name and logo. The site we are creating is a person website as it mostly talks about me and my tutorials for now. So, we will select **Person** and fill in the details as shown in *Figure 15.6*:

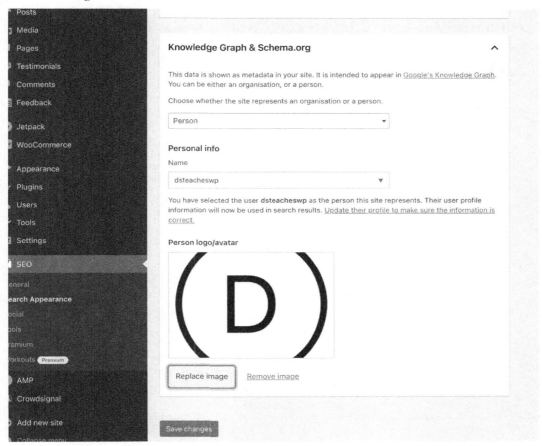

Figure 15.6: *Options entered in Knowledge Graph & Schema.org*

We will leave the other settings in "**Search Appearance**" as it is. Yoast SEO already sets most of the default settings according to best practices used by most websites. So let us now go ahead and see how to use Yoast SEO to boost the SEO of Posts and Pages on our website.

Using Yoast SEO plugin

Let us try to edit the post we created in *Chapter 6, Creating Your First Post*. If you scroll down the post, you will see that the Yoast SEO box is also present there now, as shown in the following figure:

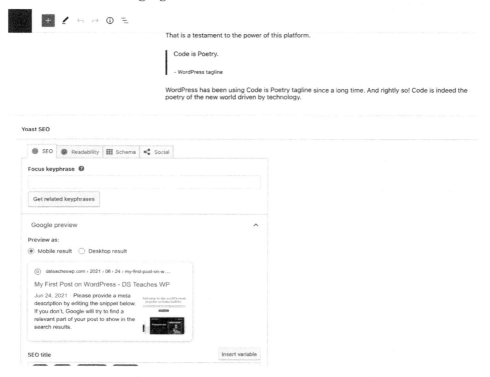

Figure 15.7: Yoast SEO plugin in a post

The following figure shows the remaining options, which you will find when you further scroll down:

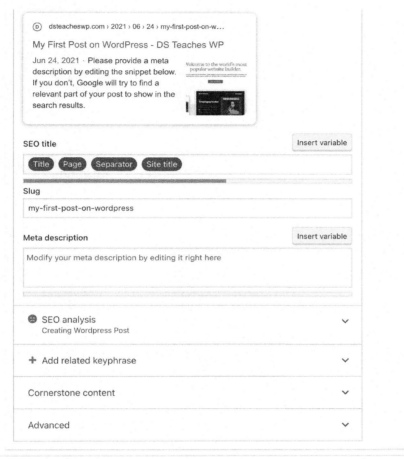

Figure 15.8: Other Yoast SEO options in a post

We will start by exploring options on the SEO tab one by one:

◆ **Focus keyphrase**: When you search for something on Google, you enter a phrase for it. That phrase contains the keyword about your query. For example, when you want to search about bicycles to buy, you may search top 10 bicycles or bicycles under 10000 INR, and so on. So, as per your requirement, your search phrase may change and that may change the search results that Google shows to you. In this field, you define what search phrase you feel would be most relevant to your post. This will help Google rank your post for those keywords, and even the Yoast SEO plugin will provide you feedback for improvement based on that.

◆ **Google Preview**: Here, you can see how this post will look when it appears in the search results of Google. You can either see its mobile result preview or the desktop one. As you make changes in the fields of the plugin, your preview may change accordingly.

◆ **SEO Title**: SEO Title consists of variables. The default title is defined in the Yoast SEO settings; however, we can also change it for a particular post. The order of variables here puts the title of the post first followed by a "-" separator and then the title of our site. Thus, you can see the same title when you check the preview of the post in search results.

◆ **Slug**: Slug is generally the last part of the URL of your post. It uniquely identifies the post on your website. WordPress automatically creates the URL for you, but you can also change that using this option. However, it is not required.

◆ **Meta Description**: When you see a search result on Google, there is often some text below the title of the search result. You can see the same in your preview as well. The text that comes along with your search result below the title is your meta description. You can define that here. Having a catchy meta description ensures that you get more clicks and, therefore, more traffic.

◆ **SEO Analysis**: You can click the SEO Analysis option below the meta description, and it will provide you recommendations to improve the SEO of your post. You can check the SEO recommendations for our post in *Figure 15.9*. It is quite low now, but we didn't work on SEO earlier. So, we can take the feedback from Yoast and improve the SEO of our post:

☹ SEO analysis   ︿
   Creating Wordpress Post

+ Add synonyms
+ Add related keyphrase

| Did you know Yoast SEO Premium also analyses the different word forms   **Go Premium! ▶**
| of your keyphrase, like plurals and past tenses?

Analysis results

︿ Problems (6)

● Outbound links: No outbound links appear in this page. Add some!

● Internal links: No internal links appear in this page, make sure to add some!

● Keyphrase density: The focus keyphrase was found 0 times. That's less than the recommended minimum of 2 times for a text of this length. Focus on your keyphrase!

● Meta description length: No meta description has been specified. Search engines will display copy from the page instead. Make sure to write one!

● Text length: The text contains 156 words. This is far below the recommended minimum of 300 words. Add more content.

● Keyphrase in title: not all the words from your keyphrase "Creating Wordpress Post" appear in the SEO title. For the best SEO results, write the exact match of your keyphrase in the SEO title, and put the keyphrase at the beginning of the title.

︿ Improvements (3)

● Image Keyphrase: images on this page do not have alt attributes that reflect the topic of your text. Add your keyphrase or synonyms to the alt tags of relevant images!

● Key phrase in introduction: your key phrase or its synonyms appear in the first paragraph of the copy, but not within one sentence. Fix that!

● SEO title width: The SEO title is too short. Use the space to add keyphrase variations or create compelling call-to-action copy.

︿ Good results (4)

● Images: good job!

● Keyphrase length: Good job!

● Previously used keyphrase: You've not used this keyphrase before, very good.

● Keyphrase in slug: More than half of your keyphrase appears in the slug. That's great!

Figure 15.9: *SEO analysis recommendations*

You can skip other options on the SEO tab as they are not that useful for us now. We will now explore the **Readability** tab shown in the following figure:

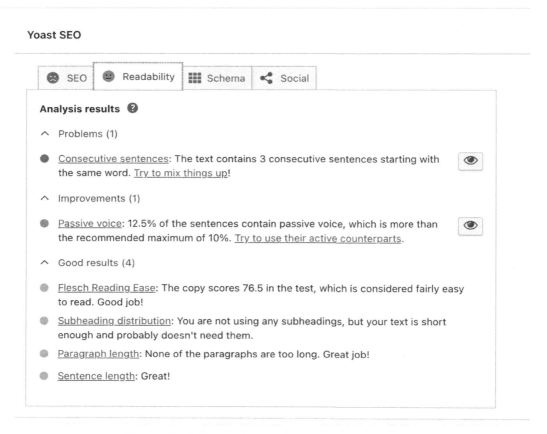

Figure 15.10: Readability analysis recommendations

The **Readability** tab provides an analysis of how easy it is for our readers to read our content. It is very important to keep our content engaging and easy to read for our readers for good SEO. That is so because Google would only want to rank such websites that have good content. Our current Readability score is fine with some room for improvement.

We can skip the schema tab as its default settings are already perfect for WordPress posts and move to the **Social** tab shown in the following figure:

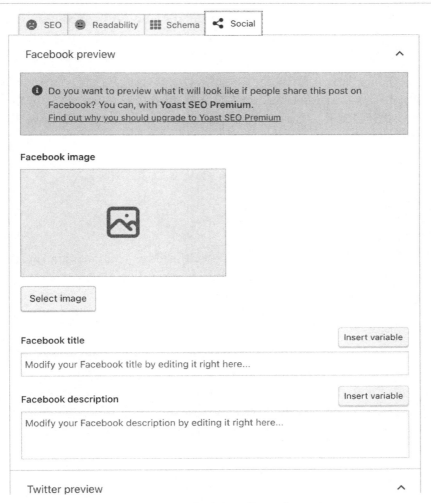

Figure 15.11: Social media configuration

Till now, we have optimized our content for search engines, but it is also important to optimize it for social media websites. And believe it or not, social media websites do affect your search engine rankings as well. This is because when people interact more with you on social media, they are well aware of your brand. Hence, they would click on your website when its recommendation comes on Google. This will help Google know people like going to your website, thereby increasing your rankings even further.

On the social media tab, you can define how your post will show up on *Facebook*. When people share your post on Facebook, Facebook automatically fetches the title, description, and image of the post (try sharing a link on Facebook and see how Facebook automatically fetches these details). So you can define what title, image, and description should Facebook show for your post. You can do the same for Twitter as well. To enter these details, you can use variables like on the SEO tab or even enter the details directly.

To save the settings you have added, simply update the post. You should also configure Yoast SEO for all the pages that you create. You will have the same options there as well.

Recap

SEO is very important for any website today. You can use the learnings from this chapter to efficiently optimize your website for search engines to get website visitors. Also, we hope that configuring the Yoast SEO plugin gave you an idea of how plugins enhance your website with completely new options.

There were no SEO-related options on our WordPress website earlier. Adding the Yoast SEO plugin not only enabled us to add options throughout the website, it also enabled us to optimize each post and page individually. In the next chapter, we will cover a new plugin that will allow us to create more interactive pages much easily on WordPress.

Points to Remember

- SEO stands for Search Engine Optimization. As the name says, it means optimizing your website for search engines.

- Search engines help you get website visitors for free. The website visitors that come from search engines are generally also interested in the kind of content your website provides.

- Start SEO data optimization button on Yoast SEO settings sets up your website for SEO and automatically does all the initial optimization.

- Select the type of website in the knowledge graph section. If your website is about yourself, then your website represents a person, but if it is for your business then it represents an organization.

- When you search for something on Google, you enter a phrase for it. The phrase that is most closely related to your post would be your Focus Keyphrase.

- Slug is generally the last part of the URL of your post. It uniquely identifies the post on your website.

- The text that comes along with your search result below the title is your meta description.

- The Readability tab provides an analysis of how easy it is for our readers to read our content.

- To save the Yoast SEO settings you have added, simply update the post.

Multiple Choice Questions

1. **SEO stands for:**
   a. Search Engine Overall
   b. Smart Engine Optimization
   c. Search Engine Optimization
   d. None of these

2. **Meta description is:**
   a. The title that Google shows in the search results
   b. Text that Google shows below the title in search results
   c. The content of your post
   d. None of these

3. **Identify the slug in this URL - https://dsteacheswp.com/2021/06/24/my-first-post-on-wordpress/**
   a. **https://dsteacheswp.com/2021/06/24/my-first-post-on-wordpress/**
   b. **https://dsteacheswp.com**
   c. 2021/06/24
   d. my-first-post-on-wordpress

4. **Focus Keyphrase is:**

   a. Title of your post

   b. The most close keyword that you expect users will use to search your post

   c. Same as meta description

   d. None of these

5. If your school asks you to create a website for your school, then which option will you select in Knowledge Graph & Schema.org section:

   a. Person – Because you are making it

   b. Organization – Because it is for your school

   c. Can be both

   d. None of these

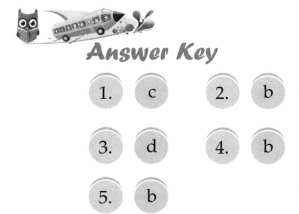

Answer Key

1. c	2. b
3. d	4. b
5. b	

Take it Further

o Check different recommendations that come for SEO Analysis and Readability Analysis on your post and fix them. Then see how the analysis recommendations change.

o Try sharing a link on Facebook and see how it fetches information of the link automatically.

Chapter 16

Adding Animation and Interaction to Your Pages

*W*e covered pages in *Chapter 8, Creating a Page*. But what if we say we can do more than what we learned there? Well, as we had discussed before, plugins are available for anything on WordPress. And as it happens, there is a plugin that enables you to add animation to your posts and pages. So we will install that plugin in this chapter and add some animation to our content.

Setting up the animate plugin

Let us begin by installing our plugin. Hover over plugins on your left WordPress sidebar menu and click on **Add New**. Type Animate in the search box, and you will get the results as shown in *Figure 16.1*:

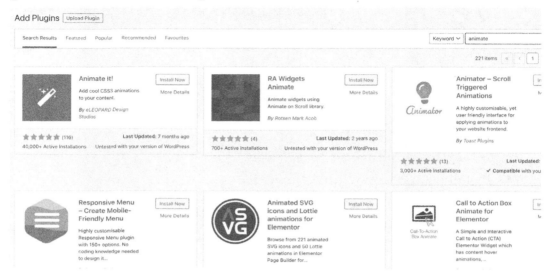

Figure 16.1: Searching Animate plugin

Click on **Install Now** button for **Animate It**. Once it is installed, the **Install Now** button will change to **Activate** button. Click on the **Activate** button too to activate the plugin on your website.

That's it. The Animate plugin is now ready for use. "**Animate It**" will now come under Settings when you hover over "**Settings**" in the left sidebar menu on your dashboard. We need not change any settings for it as its default settings will be good for us.

We will now learn how to use this plugin on our pages.

Revamping the homepage

Even though we have customized our website to a great extent, our homepage still looks a bit boring. So let us use animation on our homepage to make it more vibrant.

Hover over pages, and click on **All Pages** on your left sidebar menu. Then click on **Home**, and we get the following page:

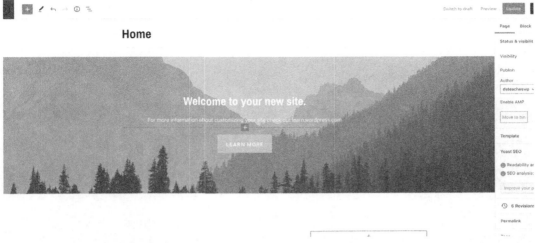

Figure 16.2: Homepage in editor

Before we add any animation, let us first change the image on our homepage. Then, we will replace it with a better image relevant to our website. To replace the image, we click on the image and then hover over **Replace**, as shown here:

Figure 16.3: Replacing the image

We will click on **Upload** and upload our image. Here is how it looks after replacing the image:

Figure 16.4: Image Preview

Let us also edit the content on the image, as shown in the following figure:

Home

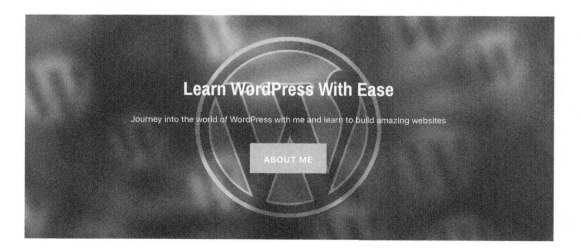

Figure 16.5: Editing the content on the image

We have edited the content and have also changed the button text. The button is now linked with the **About Me** page on the website. Just as we had learned in *Chapter 8, Creating a Page*, to edit any part, we simply have to click on it and then enter our content when the edit option comes up.

Let us update the page and check how it looks on the website. Refer to the following figure:

Figure 16.6: *The updated page on the website*

It looks much better than it did earlier and is quite relevant to our website. Now, we will add animation to make the page more lively.

Using Animate It plugin

Let us begin by adding animation to the image section on this page. Click on the image. You will find a new Animate symbol in the options now. The animate symbol has been highlighted in a red circle in *Figure 16.7*:

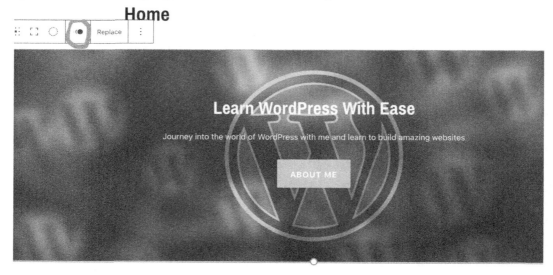

Figure 16.7: *Animate option*

Clicking on the Animate symbol will show options, as you can see in *figure 16.8*:

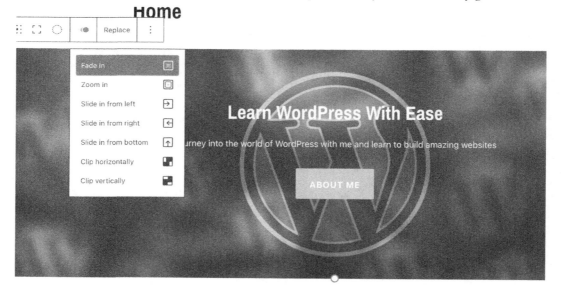

Figure 16.8: *Different animation options*

You have the option of applying the following animations:

◆ **Fade in**: The image section will be faded out initially and will gradually fade in.

◆ **Zoom in**: The image section will be small and will keep zooming till it occupies its full place.

◆ **Slide in from left**: The image section will slide in from the left side of the screen.

◆ **Slide in from right**: The image section will slide in from the right side of the screen.

◆ **Slide in from bottom**: The image section will slide in from the bottom section.

◆ **Clip horizontally**: The image section will be divided into two halves horizontally, and one half will come from the left side, whereas the other half will slide in from the right side.

◆ **Clip vertically**: The image section will be divided into two halves vertically, and one half will come from the top side, whereas the other half will slide in from the bottom side.

You can also hover over each animation effect to see how it will look. The preview of the animation will be shown in a small box in *Figure 16.9*:

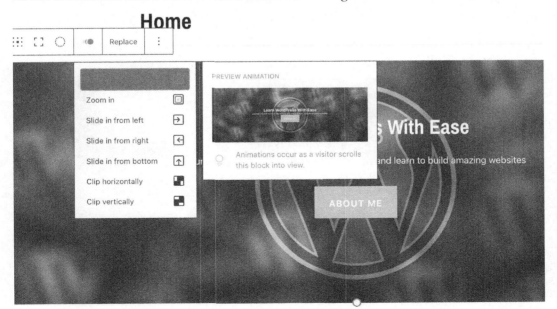

Figure 16.9: Preview of animation

We will select the `Fade in` animation for this image section. After doing that, the image on the website homepage will fade in from nothing to the full image when we open the page.

We can also apply animations to different texts on the page. To apply animation to any text area, click on it. For example, let us click on the "`Latest from the Blog`" text, as you can see in the following figure:

Figure 16.10: Adding animation to text

When you do that, you wouldn't find any animate symbol here. So, what do we do? This text area has text characters that are independent of each other. So, to apply animation to it, we will first have to group them together.

Click on the three-dot symbol at the end, and you will get more options. One of those options will be "`Group`", which is highlighted in *Figure 16.11*:

Figure 16.11: Grouping the text

After grouping it, the group of these text characters will be auto-selected. And you will have the animate symbol present there now, as shown in the following figure:

Figure 16.12: Adding animation to grouped text

Click on the animate symbol and let us select the **Slide in from left** animation for it.

Your text will now slide in from the left side of the screen. That is how you can apply animation to different parts of your page. Similarly, you can apply animation to your posts too. Although you wouldn't want to put in so much effort for every post, it is definitely worth it for static pages.

We revamped our homepage in this chapter and made it look more vibrant and relevant to the theme of our website. We also learned how to use the Animate It plugin to add animation to our pages. There are also other animation plugins, which you can try.

In the next chapter, we will cover a few more plugins that will enable us to extend the functionality of our website.

Points to Remember

- Your website's homepage should have images relevant to the theme of your website.

- Animate It plugin supports the following kinds of animation: Fade in, zoom in, slide in from left, slide in from right, slide in from bottom, clip horizontally, and clip vertically.

- To add animation to texts, you have to group them first and then apply animation to the group.

- Animate It plugin can be used on posts too.

Multiple Choice Questions

1. Zoom in animation does the following for an image:

    a. Image will appear full at the start and then slowly disappear

    b. Image will be completely transparent and not visible at the start and then slowly appears

    c. Image will be very small at the start and then gradually become big

    d. Image will be very big at the start and then gradually become small

2. Animation can be added to texts too:

    a. True

    b. False

3. Animate plugin can be used only on pages:

    a. True

    b. False

Answer Key

Take it Further

o   Try adding animation to other areas on your pages.

o   Experiment with animation on posts too.

o   Try using another Animation plugin and see how it works.

Chapter
17

Few More Popular Plugins

Structure Bot

In this chapter, we will discuss the following topics:

◆ Finding useful plugins
◆ Plugin to add popup
◆ Plugin to enable website visitors to share your content
◆ Plugin to add WhatsApp chat
◆ Other plugins you should explore on your own

$\mathcal{W}$e have so far covered two plugins. By now, you must have understood how plugins add new functionality to our website. You must have also learned how you can configure plugins and how their settings or features may change as per their use case. In this chapter, we will cover a few more plugins to make you feel more confident in using plugins on your own.

Objective Bot

At the end of this chapter, you will:

◆ Feel confident in trying out new plugins and setting them up on your website

Finding useful plugins

Have you noticed how we have found plugins till now? We discovered a use case, typed it in the search box, and installed and activated the plugin. But there may be multiple plugins of the same type that can appear in search results. In such cases, you can check the reviews to compare those plugins and install the one that best matches your requirements.

So what if you are new to website development and can't imagine different use cases? In that scenario, it would be useful to just go to the plugins page and check out trending or featured plugins. Such plugins are used by most of the websites and would definitely solve some of the most common use cases.

For example, the first plugin that we installed was Yoast SEO. That plugin is used by almost all WordPress websites and is very important for SEO. But if you do not know about SEO, you may never imagine that use case. So, it is a good idea also to check out what problems most popular plugins are solving and decide whether you want to address them too.

Plugin to add popup

Popup is that information or content that pops up on the page over all the other content when the user lands on the website. It is quite useful to share important information that you want your users to go through before using your website. Many websites also use it to ask users to mandatorily login. To add a popup plugin to our website, let's search popup in the search box, as shown here:

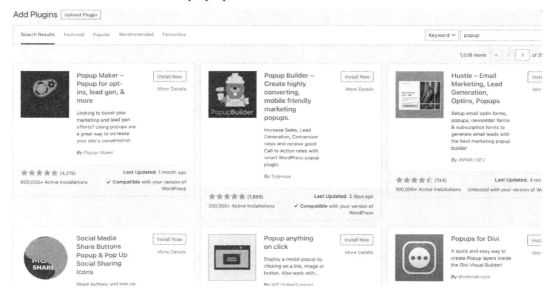

Figure 17.1: Search results for a popup plugin

The first plugin **Popup Maker** that has come up for our search query seems to solve our problem. It also has good reviews and is being actively used by 600,000+ websites.

We will install and activate it. After activating the popup, you will be taken to a page where you will be told about different cases in which we can use the popup. Let us go ahead and create our first popup. To create a popup, click on **Create Popup**, after hovering over **Popup Maker** on your sidebar menu on the WordPress dashboard, as shown in the following figure:

Figure 17.2: Create a new Popup page

The first field is **Popup Name**. You can enter a name here that will help you remember what the popup is about. As you create more popups, you may not remember what each one of them does. So, you can add a memorable name here and this name can only be seen by you.

Popup Title is the title of the popup that your website visitors will see. Then we have a big text area to add content for the popup. You can start writing the content there, and you can even add images using the **Add Media** button. You can try using the "**Add Poll**" or "**Add Contact Form**" option.

Once we have the content ready for popup as shown in *Figure 17.3*, we can then define the settings for the popup. These settings will define on which page the popup would come, when it would come, and how it would appear:

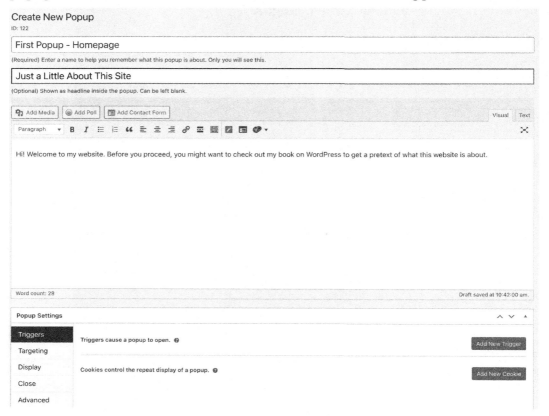

Figure 17.3: Create a Popup page with filled fields

We have created our first popup to let our website visitors know that this website is connected to the book you are reading. This way, they will know that to properly understand what this website is about, they will have to read this book first.

Let us define the settings now. In the **Triggers** tab, click on **Add New Trigger**. When you click on that button, you will have three options to select as trigger:

◆ **Click Open**: It is to be used when you want the popup to open on click of an item. For example, you can open the popup when someone clicks on a button on your website.

◆ **Time Delay/Auto Open**: It is used when you want the popup to open on its own immediately or after some time delay.

◆ **Form Submission**: It will open the popup after a user has filled a form on your website.

We will select the second option for our use case as we want our popup to open on its own. You will also have a checkbox there to select whether you want to show popup to users who have seen it once or not. You can check or uncheck that option depending on your requirements. In the next step, we will be asked what time we want to set for the popup to show up. We will select 0ms as we want it to show immediately without any time delay.

Let us go to the **Targeting** tab now (refer to *Figure 17.4*). Here you can select the pages on which the popup should show. We just want to show the popup on our homepage for now, so we will select **Homepage**. You can also disable this popup on mobile or tablets. We don't want to do that, so we will leave those options unchecked:

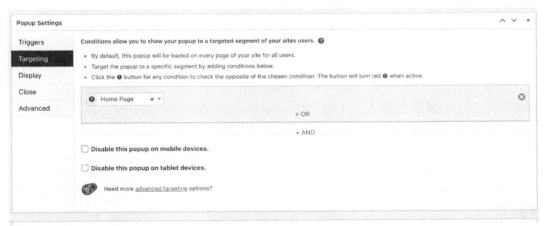

Figure 17.4: *Targeting options for Popup*

Moving to the **Display** tab (*Figure 17.5*) now, here we can choose how our popup would appear:

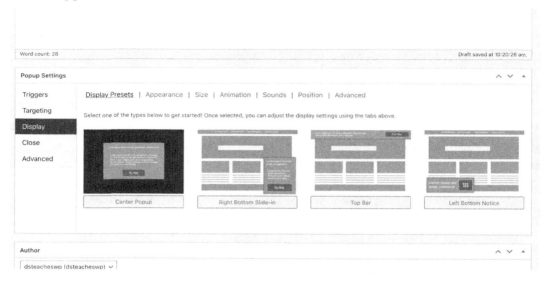

Figure 17.5: Display options for Popup

You can also configure size, animation, sounds, and more for the popup by clicking the relevant tab on the top horizontal header menu of this section. We will only configure where the popup would appear right now. Let us go with the Center Popup option.

In the next tab, "**Close**", you can configure how your close button will look. The last tab, "**Advanced**", is not required for our popups, although feel free to experiment with it.

The popup on our website homepage looks like this:

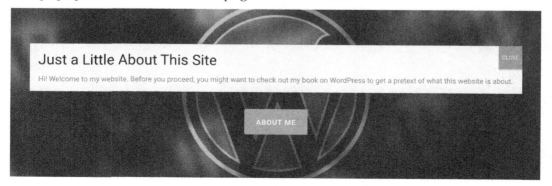

Figure 17.6: Popup on the website

Our visitors can close the popup by clicking on the **CLOSE** button. This is how you can add popups to your website. You can go ahead and add more popups with different configurations.

We will now add a Share plugin to our website.

Enabling website visitors to share your content

What do you do when you like an article on the Internet or even a picture on Instagram? You share it with your friends. And this is how that article or picture gets viral because everyone keeps sharing it with their friends. If you too want such a virality on your website, you would have to enable sharing of your content.

We can do that with a share plugin. Go to plugins and search share, and you will get something like that shown in the following figure:

Figure 17.7: Search results for share plugin

In the search results, WordPress will show you Jetpack, which is already installed on our website. And this is why if you go to one of your posts, you can see the share option present there already. But let us try to configure it a bit. Click on **Configure**, and you will get the following page:

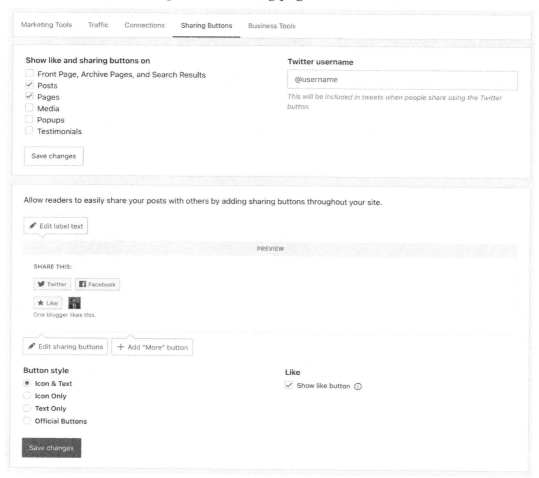

Figure 17.8: *Configuration Page of share plugin*

You can configure where the share buttons will be shown on our website. You can also change the text of buttons and its look by selecting **Icon & Text**, **Icon** only, **Text only**, or **Official Buttons**. We will go with the official buttons, and we will show it only on our posts.

You can also add more buttons by clicking on the Edit Sharing buttons. When you click on it, you will get a box to add more social media websites as follows:

Figure 17.9: *Different social media network websites you can add*

We have added *LinkedIn* and *WhatsApp* too to our list. After we have saved our changes, this is how it looks on one of our posts:

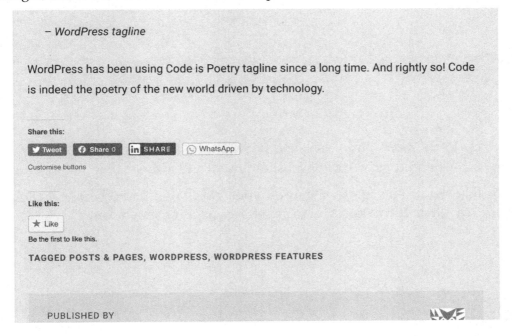

Figure 17.10: *Preview on website*

Our website visitors can now easily share our content on *Twitter*, *Facebook*, *LinkedIn*, and *WhatsApp*.

Enabling your users to chat with you on WhatsApp

There will be times when your users want to reach out to you to provide a few suggestions or need some support. In such cases, it would be great if they could somehow chat with you. And what better way to chat than on WhatsApp?

We will now install a plugin using which your website visitors can send you a message on WhatsApp.

Go to **Add Plugins** page and search "WhatsApp" in the search box as shown in the following figure:

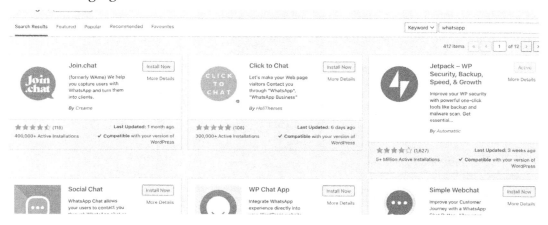

Figure 17.11: Search results for WhatsApp chat plugin

The **Click to Chat** plugin seems to be good as it has a great rating and is also being actively used by 300,000+ websites. Install and activate that plugin.

After that, go to the sidebar menu on your WordPress dashboard and click on **Click To Chat**. It will take you to its settings page, as shown here:

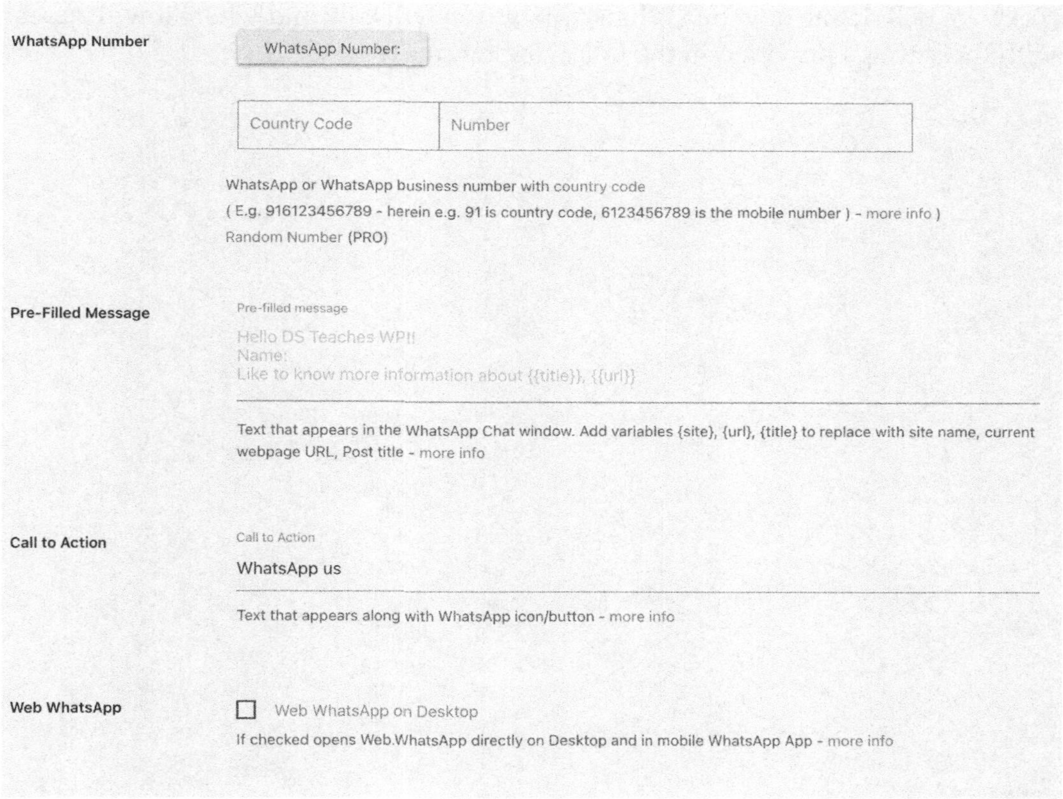

WhatsApp Number

> WhatsApp Number:

Country Code	Number

WhatsApp or WhatsApp business number with country code
(E.g. 916123456789 - herein e.g. 91 is country code, 6123456789 is the mobile number) – more info)
Random Number (PRO)

Pre-Filled Message

Pre-filled message

Hello DS Teaches WP!!
Name:
Like to know more information about {{title}}, {{url}}

Text that appears in the WhatsApp Chat window. Add variables {site}, {url}, {title} to replace with site name, current webpage URL, Post title – more info

Call to Action

Call to Action

WhatsApp us

Text that appears along with WhatsApp icon/button – more info

Web WhatsApp

☐　Web WhatsApp on Desktop

If checked opens Web.WhatsApp directly on Desktop and in mobile WhatsApp App – more info

Figure 17.12: Settings page of the chat plugin

Enter your country code and WhatsApp number there. The Country Code for India is "91".

A **Pre-Filled Message** is a message that would be automatically configured for your users when they try to send a message to you. They can change it if they want. You can also use variables in this message, such as "title", which will automatically add the title of the page in the message. **Call to Action** is the text that will be shown along with the WhatsApp button.

We will tick **Web WhatsApp** so that when users open our website on their laptop, they are taken to the WhatsApp website. On mobile devices, they will be taken to WhatsApp app.

Next, we will define how our WhatsApp button will look and where it will appear with the settings provided in the following figure:

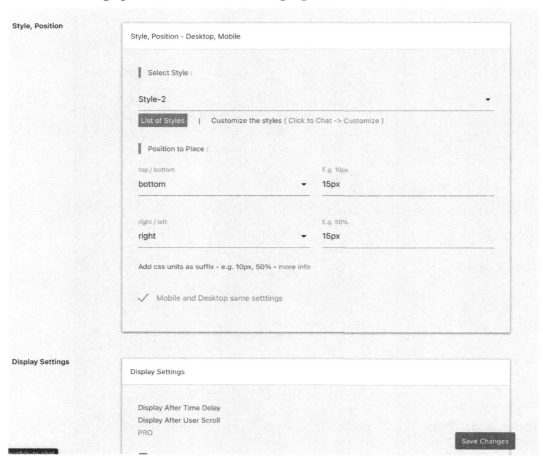

Figure 17.13: Style and display settings

There are a lot of preset styles from which you can choose. You can customize these styles by going to Customize section of **Click to Chat** by hovering over it in the sidebar menu. You should try to do this on your own as an exercise.

In the **Display Settings**, you can choose on what pages and devices will the WhatsApp button show. We have selected the option to show it on all pages and all devices.

Now, let us check the button on our website. It appears on the bottom right side of all our pages, as shown in the following figure:

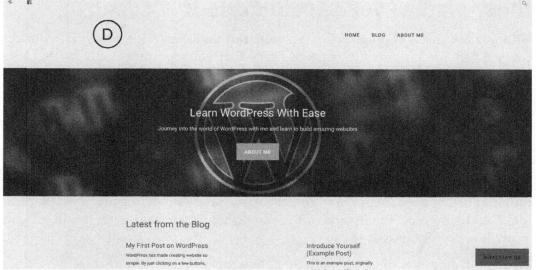

Figure 17.14: *Preview of WhatsApp Us button on the website*

You can change the design of the button by checking out the Customize section of the plugin. Now, all our users can easily contact us by clicking on the **WHATSAPP US** button. And they will be taken to WhatsApp with our pre-filled message as in the following figure:

Figure 17.15: *WhatsApp app with our pre-filled message*

That's it. You have made it very easy for your website visitors to reach out to you through your website.

Other plugins you should explore

We have covered 4-5 plugins in this book. But there are a lot more that you can cover. There are plugins for every use case that you can imagine. Now that you feel confident installing, activating, and configuring plugins, you should check out a few more.

One cannot really define how to configure a plugin. As you have seen, each plugin comes with different configuration options, which depend on the use case solved by that plugin.

Although all these configurations are generally very intuitive after setting up the plugins in this book, you shouldn't face any problem setting up new plugins. Make sure you read the details of the plugin by clicking on it, as it will let you know how to configure it.

We would suggest you also try out the following plugins on your own:

◆ **Comments** – wpDiscuz: This plugin will allow you to extend the comment functionality of your website. It comes with fancy layouts, which you can use to increase the visual appeal of your comments section. It will also make commenting fast on your website.

◆ **Smart Slider 3**: Add sliders to your website with this plugin.

◆ **Easy Google Fonts**: This plugin will allow you to try many new fonts for text on your website.

◆ **WordPress Popular Posts**: A plugin that displays the most popular posts. It comes with the various design themes and sorting logic.

The preceding four plugins will help you get started configuring plugins on your own.

We added/modified three plugins in this chapter. As you configure more plugins, you will feel more confident. Then you can go ahead and discover new plugins on your own and add them to your website.

In the next chapter, we will launch our website and explore what you can do next in your journey as a website developer.

Points to Remember

- Pop-up is the information that pops up on the page over all the other content when the user lands on the website.

- There are three different triggers available for popup – Click Open, Time Delay, and Form Submission.

- For the popup plugin, you can select pages on which it will be shown in the Targeting tab.

- You can select the social media websites where users can share your content in the Jetpack share plugin.

- Pre-Filled Message is the message that would be automatically filled for your users when they are taken to WhatsApp in the WhatsApp chat plugin.

- You can configure the design of the WhatsApp Us button in the Customize section of the plugin.

Multiple Choice Questions

1. What is the difference between popup and normal content on your website?
   a. Popup comes on top of other content on your website
   b. Popup comes behind other content on your website
   c. Popup comes below the content on your website
   d. None of these

2. To open the popup as soon as someone opens our page, what time delay will you set?
   a. 10 ms
   b. 0 ms
   c. 100 ms
   d. Any of these

3. Popup plugin will only show popup on the homepage.

    a. True

    b. False

4. Share plugin does not:

    a. Help you make your content go viral

    b. Make it easier for you to write content

    c. Enable your users to share content

    d. Do any of these

5. In Figure 17.15, the text that is being sent as a message is an example of:

    a. Call to action setting

    b. Style setting

    c. Pre-Filled Message setting

    d. None of these

Answer Key

1. a   2. b

3. b   4. b

5. c

Take it Further

o Install, activate, and configure the four plugins suggested at the end of this chapter. After that, try exploring and adding new plugins on your own.

Chapter 18

Launching Your Website and What to Do Next ?

Structure Bot

In this chapter, we will discuss the following topics:

◆ Launching the website

◆ Summarizing our learnings

◆ Technologies you can explore further

As the book went along, we built our website and made it better in each chapter. We also added new functionalities to it using plugins. And now, we have a working website that looks great! In this chapter, we will launch our website for the world, and we will also discuss what you can do next in your web development journey.

Objective Bot

At the end of this chapter, you will:

◆ Learn to launch your website on the Internet

◆ Be aware of other technologies that you can explore to advance your web development skills further

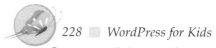

Launching the website

So far, whenever you opened your website, you must have seen a message saying that your website hasn't been launched, as shown in the following figure:

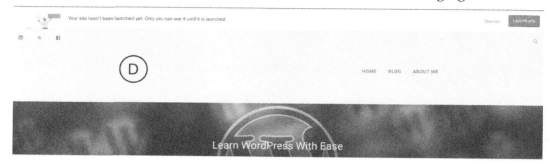

Figure 18.1: *Website launch message*

The message at the top of the figure says: Only you can see it until it is launched. You are able to see this website because you are logged in on your WordPress dashboard in another tab. If you sign out and then open the website, you will see a **Coming Soon** message as shown in the following figure:

Figure 18.2: *Coming Soon page*

This is what your website visitors must be seeing right now. To launch your website, click on the **Launch Site** button on the top right in *Figure 18.1*. After clicking on the button, wait for a couple of minutes, and then you will get a message, saying "*You launched your site*", as shown here:

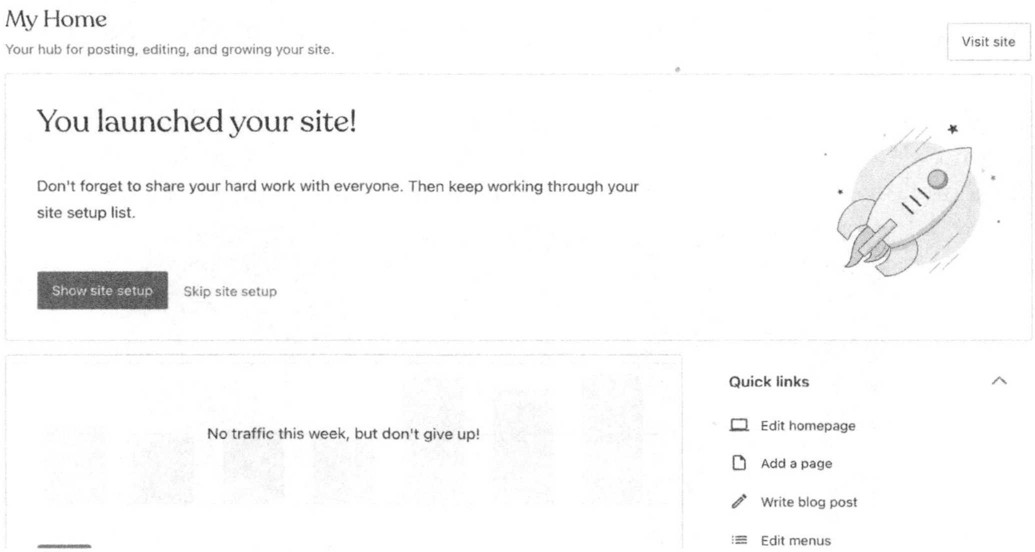

My Home
Your hub for posting, editing, and growing your site.

Visit site

You launched your site!

Don't forget to share your hard work with everyone. Then keep working through your
site setup list.

Show site setup Skip site setup

No traffic this week, but don't give up!

Quick links

🖥 Edit homepage

📄 Add a page

✏ Write blog post

☰ Edit menus

Figure 18.3: Page you will see after the successful launch

We have already set up our site, so we need not do it again. This is it. We have
launched our site on the Internet, and any user can access it.

Go ahead and share your website with your friends. Take their feedback and keep
making the website better.

Summarizing our learnings

From understanding the fundamentals of web development in *Chapter 1, WordPress
and Subway – Understanding WordPress with the Help of Sandwiches*, to adding
advanced features to our website with plugins in the last chapter, we have come a
long way. During our journey, we covered the following topics:

- Basic understanding of WordPress and web development in general
- Configuring our website and its domain
- Creating content with posts and pages
- Making website look more attractive with themes
- Customizing theme to enhance its functionalities and look
- Using menus and widgets
- And finally, understanding plugins to add more features to our website
  such as animations

The previously mentioned points summarize what we have learned so far. By now, you must have gained an intuitive understanding of WordPress and how its different components work.

But you need to understand one thing. The world of web development is very dynamic. No two websites are the same. Even the same website would load differently on different devices, as you can see in the illustration in *Figure 18.4*:

Figure 18.4: Illustration showing the same website on different devices

What we have covered in this book is one way of setting up the website. There can be many more ways. Although the idea to do so was to familiarize you with the different options available on the WordPress dashboard. You can select a different theme, add other plugins, customize the same theme differently, and many more things. With every different configuration you do in your WordPress setting, your theme, or even a plugin you add, you change something that makes your website different.

The final website that you create would depend on your imagination and creativity. Still, the learnings that you had in this book would prove to be instrumental in helping you set up the site. That is so because the fundamentals would remain the same. No matter how different your final website is, it will still be built with a theme, and its content will still be created with posts and pages.

Technologies you can explore further

In *Chapter 1, WordPress and Subway – Understanding WordPress with the Help of Sandwiches*, we had covered three different ways of website development:

Readymade website builders: These are the tools that easily allow you to create a website with a click of a few buttons. These tools, however, do not allow you to do much customization.

WordPress-like CMS systems: WordPress-like tools allow you the best of both worlds. They make the process of development very easy and at the same time also allow you to do customizations and add new features.

Making everything from scratch: This is where we make use of technologies like HTML, CSS, backend language, and more to create our website completely on our own. This gives us complete control over our website.

In this book, we have laid the foundation for using WordPress. As we have discussed earlier, there is still a lot for you to explore. There are many themes and plugins that you can explore, and when combined with your creativity, you can create a number of different kinds of websites.

WordPress.com versus WordPress.org

We have covered *WordPress.com* in this book, but there is one more type of WordPress that you can explore – *WordPress.org*, which is shown in the following figure:

Figure 18.5: WordPres.org

WordPress.org is the open-source self-hosted version of WordPress. To understand what this means, let us first understand Open Source. Open-Source technologies are those technologies whose code is not private and is made publicly available. One can also modify that code and distribute it separately.

For example, as *WordPress.org* is an open source platform, we can take the *WordPress.org* code and create our own WordPress-like tool. We can make some changes to it and name it differently. We too would have a CMS tool of our own then! Other people can even use our tool instead of WordPress if they find it more helpful.

Being open source, it also provides much more control over your website and in fact is more closely related to the third type of website development that we discussed previously. This is so because we can change the code of WordPress too if required, therefore, being able to control everything from scratch. Even if we don't do that, we still have more control. On a WordPress website, which hasn't been upgraded, WordPress can place ads as they wish. These things won't be a problem on WordPress.org. You will decide what goes up on your website and what does not.

To build a website using *WordPress.org*, either you can install it on a blank server or you can go for such hosting services that automatically do the installation for you. You can check out hosting services, such as Bluehost, Hostgator, Namecheap, and more for the same.

As it is open source, you don't even have to pay on *WordPress.org* to use plugins. However, you will have to pay some charges to your hosting service provider for using their server to host your website.

WordPress.com, on the other hand, is a hosted version of WordPress by the creators of WordPress. They make it very easy to build a website as you don't have to deal with hosting service providers separately. You can just sign up and get started.

However, most of the options and dashboards for both *WordPress.com* and *WordPress.org* will almost feel the same. So, you wouldn't have any problem utilizing your learning in this book on *WordPress.org* too.

Writing your own code

Once you have practiced enough and become comfortable with WordPress, you can take the next step in the world of web development. If you remember, in the customization options that we covered in *Chapter 10, Customizing Your Theme*, there was an option to add additional CSS. This customization option allows you to directly add CSS code to your WordPress website that will alter the design accordingly.

After you are comfortable enough with *WordPress.com* and *WordPress.org*, you can start learning CSS and make use of this option. While learning CSS, it would also be a good idea to learn HTML from an online course or a book so that your fundamentals are clear. That would then allow you to imagine how WordPress automatically creates the page for you when you use options on its dashboard. You will be able to understand what exactly happens in the code. You can see a snippet of HTML code in the following figure:

Figure 18.6: HTML code

Once you learn HTML and CSS, which are frontend technologies, you can start exploring few backend languages such as PHP. WordPress too is built using PHP. After that, you can learn a database, such as MySQL. Again, WordPress too uses MySQL.

And once you have learned all these, you can proudly call yourself a Full Stack Web Developer. It will take time, probably years, to master these skills. But it will be a fun ride.

WordPress is your gateway to the world of web development. It makes it incredibly easy for you to build a website while maintaining control over it. From here, you can pick the technologies that WordPress itself is based on and then expand your skillset. Once you start learning these technologies, you will even be able to create the Themes and Plugins installed on WordPress.

Remember, we had discussed that these plugins and themes are generally created by third-party developers. You too can become such a developer.

Recap

We have launched our website, summarized our learnings in this book, and discussed the future steps in this chapter. However, the future steps are a rough roadmap for you to follow. It can change based on your personal requirements, and you surely shouldn't jump to these advanced technologies until you have mastered WordPress.

And just theory wouldn't be enough to master it. You will have to practice and create different websites with different themes and plugins. Without practice, the knowledge you have learned so far would be of no value. The following quote by Publilius Syrus, a Latin writer from 1st century BC, is very true for any web development you do:

"Practice is the best of all instructors."

So, keep practicing, and only then will you be able to call yourself an expert WordPress developer. And with the learnings in this book, you sure can become one!

Points to Remember

- Until you launch your website, only those people who are logged into your WordPress dashboard will be able to see your website.

- With every different configuration you do in your WordPress setting, your theme, or even a plugin you add, you change something that makes your website different.

- Wordpress.org is the open-source self-hosted version of WordPress.

- After being comfortable with WordPress, you can start learning frontend technologies such as HTML and CSS. You can then cover backend technologies such as PHP and databases such as MySQL.

Multiple Choice Questions

1. **WordPress does not use:**
   - *a.* PHP
   - *b.* Golang
   - *c.* HTML
   - *d.* CSS

2. **You too can develop a theme or plugin:**
   - *a.* True
   - *b.* False

3. **You can add your own CSS in WordPress:**
   - *a.* True
   - *b.* False

Answer Key

1. b   2. a   3. a

Take it Further

Find out multiple use cases around you that can be solved using a website and create WordPress websites for them as an exercise. Here are a few ideas to get you started:

- o Create a personal website for yourself.
- o Create a blog around a subject that you love the most. Add regular content (Posts) around it.
- o Create a website for your school and show it to your teachers.
- o Create a website to sell your old books. You can make use of a plugin like Woocommerce to do this.

Printed in Great Britain
by Amazon

27053287R00143